YOUR MONEY
YOUR INVESTMENTS

YOUR MONEY YOUR INVESTMENTS

Preserving and growing your wealth in good and tough times

SECOND EDITION

DR BEN FOK CFP, ChFC

© 2020 Marshall Cavendish International (Asia) Private Limited

Design by Bernard Go Kwang Meng. Cover image by Lightspring/Shutterstock

Published by Marshall Cavendish Business
An imprint of Marshall Cavendish International

All rights reserved

No part of this publication may be reproduced, stored in a retrieval system or transmitted, in any form or by any means, electronic, mechanical, photocopying, recording or otherwise, without the prior permission of the copyright owner. Requests for permission should be addressed to the Publisher, Marshall Cavendish International (Asia) Private Limited, 1 New Industrial Road, Singapore 536196. Tel: (65) 6213 9300. E-mail: genref@sg.marshallcavendish.com
Website: www.marshallcavendish.com/genref

The publisher makes no representation or warranties with respect to the contents of this book, and specifically disclaims any implied warranties or merchantability or fitness for any particular purpose, and shall in no event be liable for any loss of profit or any other commercial damage, including but not limited to special, incidental, consequential, or other damages.

Other Marshall Cavendish Offices:
Marshall Cavendish Corporation, 800 Westchester Ave, Suite N-641, Rye Brook, NY 10573, USA • Marshall Cavendish International (Thailand) Co Ltd, 253 Asoke, 16th Floor, Sukhumvit 21 Road, Klongtoey Nua, Wattana, Bangkok 10110, Thailand • Marshall Cavendish (Malaysia) Sdn Bhd, Times Subang, Lot 46, Subang Hi-Tech Industrial Park, Batu Tiga, 40000 Shah Alam, Selangor Darul Ehsan, Malaysia

Marshall Cavendish is a registered trademark of Times Publishing Limited

National Library Board, Singapore Cataloguing in Publication Data

Name(s): Fok, Ben, 1961-.
Title: Your money your investments : preserving and growing your
    wealth in good and tough times / Dr Ben Fok.
Description: Second edition. | Singapore : Marshall Cavendish
    Business, [2020]
Identifier(s): OCN 1190518192 | 978-981-49-2806-9 (paperback)
Subject(s): LCSH: Finance, Personal. | Finance, Personal--Singapore. |
    Investments. | Investments--Singapore.
Classification: DDC 332.024--dc23

Printed in Singapore

For all readers
who want to do the right thing
for themselves, their families,
or their clients in
managing their investments.

I would like to thank God
for his blessings;
my wife, Sharon, who always encourages
me to do the things I want to do;
and my lovely children, Jeryn and Samuel,
who always keep me moving.

I Can Do All Things
Through Christ
Who Strengthens Me

Philippians 4:13

CONTENTS

PREFACE   8
To the Second Edition

PART 1
FINANCIAL PLANNING TIPS   10

1. Reality Check for Retirement Dreams   12
2. Preserving Your Nest Egg   17
3. HNWIs Need Financial Planning Even More   23
4. Retirement: How Much is Enough?   27
5. Getting Down to the ABC's of Planning for Retirement   32
6. Insurance in a Time of Uncertainty   37
7. Life Insurance as a Wealth Planning Tool   42
8. Beating Inflation at its Own Game   47
9. Interest-Only Loans: the Pros and Cons   52
10. A Pyramid Scheme that Works for You   59
11. What Customers Really Want from Their Financial Advisers?   65

PART 2
LEARNING FROM THE INVESTMENT WORLD   70

12. Getting the Most Out of Asset Allocation   72
13. Building an Investment Portfolio for Life   77
14. Your Ticket to Investing Wisely   81
15. Game for Stock Investing?   85
16. Invest Like the Rich and Your Returns May Be Better   93
17. Investing Tricks of the Wealthy   97
18. Pitfalls of Foreign Currency Investing   103
19. It's Only a Number   108
20. Making Sense of the Recent Market Rally   113
21. Compounding the Issue   118
22. Low Cost for Pure Risk   126
23. Index or Managed?   131
24. Bonds: Go It Alone or Go with a Fund?   136

PART 3
UNDERSTANDING INVESTMENT FUNDAMENTALS — 142

25 GDP and Share Prices: What's the Connection? — 144
26 Rein in Your Emotions — 149
27 About those Eggs — 155
28 Know Your Risk-Free Return — 159
29 Time to Change Strategy — 163
30 Stay Invested or Adopt Dollar-Cost Averaging — 168
31 A Boring Approach that Works — 174
32 When an Investor Burns His Finger — 179
33 The Portfolio Strategy and Your Adviser — 185
34 Shock-Proof Your Portfolio — 191
35 Have Faith in an Old Friend — 198
36 Stock Investing not Always a Gamble — 207

ABOUT THE AUTHOR — 211

PREFACE
To the Second Edition

Recent financial events have emphasised the need for understanding financial decision-making and investment strategies used by financial professionals.

In today's dynamic economic environment, it is necessary to enhance your financial planning and investment skills as every financial decision we make impacts our lives. In an environment where stakes are higher, decision making is more complex and the consequences of making wrong financial decisions are more severe.

This book grew out of my experience in engaging with clients and discovering their lack of knowledge in personal finance.

In helping you to better understand both the local and wider context of making investments, this book will raise your confidence in making personal financial and investment decisions. The articles in this book will provide practical information and prompt you to think carefully about your personal financial decisions and the long-term consequences of your decisions.

This second edition includes 15 additional articles that were published in *The Sunday Times* and *The Business Times* between 2000 and 2019.

I hope this book will not only empower you with new knowledge on how to plan your investments but also give you a passion for the fascinating subject of personal finance.

Dr Ben Fok
October 2020

Part 1

Financial planning tips

ACCUMULATING money for retirement is by far the most important reason for investing. You have invested your hard earned money all these years. When faced with a global financial crisis, what would you do to your investment portfolio? Do you panic and sell out, or do you stay calm? On the other hand, if your retirement assets are sufficient to see you through the rest of your life, how will you leave the maximum residual estate to the people you love? Have you thought about preserving what you have already accumulated? Do you wish to be a part of your family's future by leaving them a legacy?

Some people believe that life insurance is unimportant and a waste of money, but think about what will happen to your family if you were to die tomorrow. What will happen to your family's financial needs when you are gone? Will your family have sufficient money to maintain their standard of living? It does not make logical sense to think about investing for your future if you do not look after your family's financial situation should you die prematurely.

Do you believe that inflation is a major concern in the long run? You should, because inflation can harm your investment returns. It can also negatively affect your standard of living. The question, is how well prepared are you for that?

In this section, we will also examine how interest-only loans work and when they are most appropriate to use. More importantly, are they for you? We will then discuss what customers really want from their financial advisers.

01 Reality Check for Retirement Dreams
The Business Times Weekend, 17 January 2009

> As you approach retirement, you need to re-examine your risk tolerance and assess the risk of your portfolio to avoid huge losses like what we have experienced in the 2008 financial tsunami. It may also be timely to consider finding a capable financial professional to help you.

WHILE attending a dinner recently, I met an ex-uniformed officer who received his service pension five years ago. Then 50, he started investing diligently for his retirement. With a simple financial spreadsheet, he was able to calculate the funds needed in retirement, the required growth rate of his portfolio and the ideal retirement age. Over the last five years, his portfolio performed very well, growing at an average 12 per cent per annum. At such a high growth rate, he would take just eight years to achieve financial independence — when he turns 63.

He shared with me the quantitative and qualitative criteria he used to pick stocks and unit trusts. I was rather impressed by his investment strategy and believed he had the traits of a successful investor. However, he ended his story on a depressing note, saying how the current financial meltdown destroyed his retirement goal and wiped out five years of hard work and careful investing.

Coincidentally, during an investment seminar that I conducted last month, a financial adviser asked me how to explain to a trusted client that his retirement portfolio had lost 50 per cent in value. Realistically speaking, there is no use explaining that it is important to stay invested and ride out the recession. Even though the market will eventually recover, given the current state of the stock market, most clients have turned a deaf ear to such advice.

It is often the investments that grow quickly in good times that are the ones that give nasty surprises when markets drop precipitously. Many investors have lost a big chunk of their retirement funds. There could be many investors who entrusted their money with financial advisers who are facing huge losses now. If you are one of them, you are not alone. All over the world, as baby boomers grow older, they see that dangling carrot of retirement continuously moving out of reach. And millions of current retirees are wondering how much more their portfolios can take.

As an invester or financial adviser, you can't afford to stand still and take the hit. But you should ask yourself how you allowed this to happen in the first place. Instead of looking for high returns, you should have been looking to prevent a direct hit to your portfolios.

As you approach retirement, you need to re-examine your risk tolerance. Apart from understanding your risk appetite, you need to assess the risk of your portfolio. When the stock market boomed from 2005 to 2007, many retirees-to-be were overdue for a change to their investment portfolio. The percentage of stock holdings would have increased due to the bull market and the risk of the overall portfolio would have increased as well.

Let's take the ex-officer as an example. He started in 2003 with $400,000 and allocated 100 per cent to stocks and nothing to bonds. With his portfolio growing at 12 per cent, it would have been worth a respectable $705,000 after five years. If this was your portfolio, would you be comfortable with leaving 100 per cent of your nest egg in the stock market at the age of 55?

It is recommended that retirees have not more than 40 per cent of their portfolios in the stock market. If your allocation is significantly higher, consider shifting towards more conservative investments such as fixed income. For many retirees, a comfortable equity allocation would be in the 20 to 30 per cent range. Although stocks are still the best choice for building wealth over the long term, studies have shown that it is very difficult to recover if you deplete your nest egg in the early years of retirement. Of course, you don't want to sell when the market is weak (like now) and miss out on the rebound.

Financial advisers may have to rebalance their clients' portfolios and advise them to take some painful losses. They have to ensure that a client's asset allocation is appropriate for his risk tolerance, so that he can better ride out the volatility of the stock market. Investors who have had a retirement plan drawn up some time ago may have to re-assess their retirement projections. The assumptions used then may be very different from what applies today.

After you run your retirement projections, you may find that you can no longer retire as early as you hoped. Do not despair. For a start, look at your debt; go through your recent credit card statements and cheque book to see what expenses you can cut. Know how much interest you are paying on credit cards and other types of debt. If possible, restructure those debt payments so that you pay less interest.

You may consider refinancing your mortgage over a longer period at a lower interest rate so that your monthly payment is reduced. You may even have to save more or make other big sacrifices, such as spending less money in retirement. If you need to work longer, then do so. It might even be healthier to do what you enjoy than to retire completely. Lastly, re-examine your retirement expectations. You might, for instance, find that you get as much enjoyment from simpler activities that don't cost very much.

During a bull run, any investor can look like an investment genius. While you may have been comfortable being a do-it-yourself investor when times were good, you may find yourself in a difficult position today. It may be time to consider finding a capable financial professional to help you. For those of you who already have a financial adviser, consider whether he has taken the time to talk to you regarding re-positioning your portfolio in this market meltdown. Most importantly, has he listened to you and understood your concerns?

This shake-up in the financial sector need not be seen in purely negative terms. Since 9/11, excess leverage has built up in the global financial system. The irresponsible use of non-traditional instruments like collateralised debt obligations (CDOs) and derivative swaps has resulted in a mountain of debt and excessive leverage. If the financial tsunami had not happened today, it would occur in the future with even worse consequences. This crisis will rid the system of excess leverage and bring prices to reasonable levels, paving the way for more sustainable growth.

While the last thing a retirement portfolio needed was a year like this, and there is cold comfort for older investors, there are some bright spots for other investors. One of them is that you can find good opportunities right now in the stock market and you don't have to take on a whole lot of risk to take advantage of them. Simple strategies like these could add to your retirement fund in your golden years.

02 Preserving Your Nest Egg
The Business Times, 26 March 2008

> After many years of hard work, you have successfully accumulated wealth and you are now looking forward to an enjoyable retirement. But how do you leave a pre-determined amount of money or legacy to your loved ones and still be able spend freely during your retirement years? A universal life insurance policy can help you achieve this as it offers greater flexibility and control over your wealth.

OFTEN, financial planning textbooks tell you that to preserve your wealth, you need to have legal protection over your assets, defer or reduce your tax payable, reduce probate, eliminate estate taxes, and finally, have a tax efficient wealth transfer to your next generation. To me, this applies only to the very wealthy and not everyone. Allow me to elaborate.

Recently, a friend of mine, John, who is 60 years old, sold the printing business he started 30 years ago and pocketed $3 million. He approached me for advice on wealth preservation.

As a financial adviser, I am prepared to use all my knowledge to advise clients on how best to preserve wealth. Naturally, with such wealth having being accumulated over many years in a structured way, every effort should be made to manage it in the most appropriate and effective manner. Essentially, it is paramount to protect what you have built up.

Instinctively, my immediate goal with John was to set up trusts, review his estate duty liabilities (this was before estate duty was abolished in 2008) and help him pass on real wealth for the benefit of his survivors. However, as I looked more into his idea of wealth preservation, I realised that it went beyond traditional strategies.

After selling his business, John estimated that he needed about $70,000 a year to maintain his standard of living throughout retirement. Being a conservative person, he did not want to risk losing his capital. He told me that he was not comfortable with equity investments because wealth can be dissipated.

John is a simple man. All he wants is to preserve the entire $3 million — or as much of it as possible — and at same time, take care of his retirement income needs. The usual strategy involves living off one's accumulated value prior to retirement and slowly depleting the principal throughout the retirement years.

John understood that if he deposited $3 million into an instrument earning 2 per cent, his money can last him well beyond age 85. But this was not what he wanted because at death, there might be nothing left for his heirs. I am not saying that this is a poor way of planning — merely that it is only suitable if a retiree decides that leaving a large inheritance isn't his primary objective. My objective is to help John minimise risk, preserve what he had built up, and at the same time create an income stream from his accumulated assets by not depleting them so that his descendants can enjoy his wealth when it is passed on. This is a plan involving both retirement planning and wealth preservation.

One strategy is for John to use his accumulated retirement funds to generate enough income/cash flow to meet his expenses throughout his retirement. For example, John's nest egg of $3 million is invested at 5 per cent. This will provide cash flow of $150,000 per annum, which is more than twice the amount he requires. So long as he does not use more than $150,000 a year, he should be able to maintain a portfolio value of $3 million available for his heirs at death.

This strategy requires John to invest in an instrument providing a yield of 5 per cent per annum. High dividend stocks, Real Estate Investment Trust (REITs) and business trusts are excellent instruments for generating such cash flow. However, taking into consideration market volatility, there is a risk that John could lose his capital, especially in a bear market. REITs and business trusts are listed on the stock exchange and are subjected to market volatility. As such, there is no guarantee that his accumulated capital could be preserved. Uncertainty abounds. Moreover, it is difficult to purchase a large quantity of these instruments at one go.

John needs an instrument that can preserve his capital and provide him with cash flow. As we explored further, we stumbled upon using universal life, a single-premium insurance policy, as an inheritance replacement tool. Universal life insurance is a valuable strategy when it comes to wealth creation and wealth preservation at death. With this type of life insurance, a single premium is deposited, creating an immediate death benefit that is guaranteed when the owner passes away. Let's see how this will work for John.

To leave $3 million for his estate, John buys a single-premium life insurance for $3 million. The premium is approximately $1 million and covers him until age 100. John can put the remaining $2 million in the bank and draw down $70,000 a year for his retirement needs. Without taking into account inflation and interest accumulated, he can draw $70,000 for 27 years until age 87. In this way, the $3 million is preserved for his estate upon his death and he can be certain that his retirement needs can be met with the $2 million parked in a risk-free environment.

Some may argue that John could invest the entire $3 million into a capital-guaranteed fixed-income instrument, such as the Singapore Government Security (SGS). To preserve the $3 million principal and produce an income stream of $70,000 (before inflation) every year, John could buy a bond that pays out an indicative yield of 2.33 per cent. Currently, SGS bonds offer such yield or higher.

At first glance, many would think it makes more sense to invest the entire capital in the bond as yields can be higher and John can receive higher cash flow each year. Do think again. The future may not always be smooth sailing. By investing in a SGS bond, John actually locks up the entire $3 million and forgoes liquidity of his capital. In the event of a major illness or any emergency, he would have no choice but to sell the bond, in which case he could incur substantial risk to the capital due to uncertain interest rates and changes to bond prices.

Furthermore, by investing in the bond, John would probably outlive the bond term and would have to buy a new bond. Again, he would be exposed to the risk that bond yields in future may not be high enough to give him sufficient cash flow to support his retirement expenses.

Some may argue that term insurance is more effective. Of course, using term insurance is more affordable but John may outlive the term of the policy. By then, to renew it will be expensive or even impossible due to a maximum age limit.

Yet others may also ask whether opting for a universal life insurance with yearly premium is a better option. For me, a single premium is preferred because universal life provides a guaranteed growth rate of about 3 to 4 per cent. If John were to invest on his own, he may not be able to grow his money at that rate without taking higher risk.

By using universal life insurance with a single premium as highlighted above, John has $2 million of liquid cash over which he has full control. He can park the money in the bank and benefit from the interest. In the event of any emergency, he can draw on that cash. John has a choice of taking some risk with the money and investing it in other assets if he wishes to. In a worst case scenario, if he outlives the $2 million cash in the bank, he can draw down the cash value of his universal life insurance policy and leave a smaller amount to his estate.

Compared with investing in a bond, a universal life insurance policy offers greater flexibility and control over your wealth.

> **Universal life insurance is a valuable strategy when it comes to wealth preservation at death. A single premium is deposited, creating an immediate death benefit that is guaranteed when the owner passes away.**

Using such a strategy, John can now leave a pre-determined amount of money to his estate with complete certainty, and spend the balance of his money today without worrying about his wealth being depleted. At the same time, he is assured that his heirs will inherit the amount he has determined. This fulfills John's objective of capital preservation and retirement needs.

03 HNWIs Need Financial Planning Even More
The Business Times, 24 October 2007

> Many wealthy people don't realise it is more important for them to have a sound strategy to keep the money they already have than to accumulate more. Think about security first, not growth. Once you've reached a point of wealth, it's more pertinent to look at the risk in investing rather than get excited about potential rewards.

A FRIEND of mine was elated when he collected a windfall of $4 million from an en bloc sale. He then proudly confessed that he had more than $4 million of investable assets and his retirement was thus assured.

At first glance, retirement planning might seem unnecessary for a High Net Worth Individual (HNWI). These are people who have net assets of at least US$1 million, excluding their home and consumables. Consider the usual assets that a HNWI would have acquired through the years: a family home, perhaps an investment property or two, one or more cars, a healthy bank account, a profitable business. So what's left to plan?

Quite a bit actually. A number of HNWIs seem to be unaware of the importance of a coordinated financial plan. Without one, many HNWIs will enter retirement with little idea of how much they can reasonably spend and how to structure a retirement portfolio that ensures they don't run out of money before they run out of breath. Another consideration is how to transfer their wealth while minimising leakages such as estate duty. There is also the issue, for some, of a business continuation plan.

While having money today makes life less stressful, increased longevity has created new anxieties about financial security in the future. I've worked with a lot of wealthy people over the years and the experience has led me to think of wealth a little differently. Wealth is more than just money; it is money used to secure a certain quality of life. So it doesn't matter how big your investment account is. If you lie awake at night worrying about your portfolio, you're not wealthy. If you wonder whether you'll run out of money, you're not wealthy. If you're not satisfied with your quality of life, you're not wealthy.

Many HNWIs have done little to protect their wealth. They haven't written a will, they don't have a trust, and they haven't named an administrator for their estate or put in place a succession business plan.

Focus on security first

To me, it is more important for HNWIs to keep the money they have than to accumulate more. For instance, my friend who pocketed the $4 million windfall is in danger of losing 5 per cent of it to taxes if he dies today. That's because a non-dutiable asset (residential property) becomes dutiable once it is converted to cash. In Singapore, estate duty rules allow an exemption of up to $9 million for residential property. But cash and other financial assets have a much lower threshold of $600,000. It does not matter whether he re-invests the sum in shares or in managed funds, it will still be dutiable. This is a timely reminder for those involved in en bloc sales to do some advance planning. (This was before estate duty was abolished in 2008.)

My advice is to think about security first — not growth. In today's bullish atmosphere, that might fall on deaf ears.

But think about it this way: if you have several million in investible assets, you have reached a point where you already have 'enough' — that is, when more money wouldn't result in a change in your lifestyle. Once you've reached this point, it is more pertinent to look at the risk in investing rather than get excited about potential rewards. That perspective can go a long way in making sure you hang on to the wealth you worked so hard to build.

Those with family businesses have other challenges, such as how to transfer the business to the next generation. Conflicts may arise when mapping out the firm's growth strategy, with the younger generation's more aggressive management style clashing with the previous generation's conservatism. Since your wealth is there to create a legacy, it's worth spending time planning how to preserve it.

Many wealthy families are also concerned about how best to raise their children so that affluence does not spoil them or dampen their drive and independence.

If you fall into any of these categories, chances are you already know money doesn't automatically solve all your problems. In fact, some of the greatest challenges you'll face come after you acquire wealth.

If you have made it as a HNWI, this is the time to take personal responsibility for your wealth. You need a clear vision of what you want to accomplish with your wealth, and be ready to address financial opportunities and challenges from an informed perspective. It is the best way to ensure continued, steady progress towards your life goals.

As you can see, wealth can create as many problems as it solves. While some people may want to explore the range of new, more complicated investment products and strategies, others may find they are well-served by the tried-and-true investment strategies. At the least, explore the options to see what works best for you.

Lastly, you may have reached a level of affluence where you need the services of a financial professional to help you preserve and transfer your wealth.

04 Retirement: How Much is Enough?
The Business Times, 18 January 2012

> Funding your retirement years comfortably is a trade-off between playing it safe, taking risks and spending prudently.

AT a family function, my 60-year-old cousin Peter asked me for my views on retirement planning. He said that over the last 35 years he has worked hard, consistently saved and prudently invested his money. When he retires in two years' time, this should provide him with a nest egg of about $500,000. As I listened to him, it seemed that he had secured his financial future. But he kept asking: "Is it really enough?"

At this age, many would expect to have a significant retirement nest egg. If they don't, they had better do something about it now.

In Singapore, our official statistics show that there are more than 300,000 individuals aged between 50 and 54 who are due to retire in 10 to 15 years' time. As a financial adviser, I often discuss this subject with my clients but often this issue is not treated as a top priority. Understandably, there are other priorities, such as children's education and mortgage repayments or other immediate needs that take precedence over retirement planning.

Given the current economic volatility, the outlook for those planning their retirement is very cloudy. Over the last two years, we have seen the cost of living here increasing yearly, making retirement more expensive and resulting in many more Singaporeans having to put off retirement for a few more years. With higher longevity and people not saving enough, the working population of those aged 60 and over will inevitably continue to rise.

In Peter's case, he and his wife are healthy and they are likely to have a long life ahead of them. So it would be a mistake to concentrate solely on what's happening now or even on what might happen months from now. Rather, they should focus on coming up with a spending and preservation plan that can assure them of enough money to live comfortably for the next 25–30 years, if not longer.

Hence, funding your retirement years is a trade-off between playing it safe, taking risks and spending prudently.

With the nest egg that Peter has accumulated, he can create a cash flow, and that is the most important consideration during his retirement. At this point, he has to set a reasonable withdrawal rate that will give him the spending cash he needs but won't deplete his nest egg too soon. Peter asked: "How much can I safely withdraw from my retirement fund every year?" It is obvious that a miscalculation could result in an involuntary return to the workforce or having insufficient funds for retirement.

To help Peter understand how much he can withdraw, I produced a table to show the number of years his money will last.

The table shows withdrawal rates ranging from 4 per cent to 13 per cent and annual growth rate of investment from 3 per cent to 12 per cent, which resembles a 100 per cent stocks to a 100 per cent bonds portfolio.

Creating a cash flow
Retirement fund plan

Withdrawal rate per year	Growth rate of investment per year									
	3%	4%	5%	6%	7%	8%	9%	10%	11%	12%
13%	8	9	9	10	11	12	13	15	17	22
12%	9	10	11	11	12	14	16	18	23	
11%	10	11	12	13	14	16	19	25		
10%	12	13	14	15	17	20	26			
9%	13	14	16	18	22	28				
8%	15	17	20	23	30					
7%	18	21	25	33						
6%	23	28	36							
5%	30	41								
4%	46									
Number of years money will last										

It also shows how many years a sum will last at various withdrawal rates and various rates of return. If the withdrawal rate and the rate of return are the same, the principal will not change. For example, when $100,000 earns 8 per cent per annum and 8 per cent is drawn, the principal stays the same. This is another strategy by which a retiree can create an income stream. So if Peter invests $500,000 in a diversified investment that can give him 5 per cent returns, he can make $25,000 per year of withdrawals without affecting his principal.

However, if $100,000 earns 4 per cent per annum ($4,000) and 8 per cent ($8,000) is withdrawn annually, the $8,000 annual income will continue for 17 years before the principal is gone.

It is important to understand that the rate of return and the withdrawal rate determine how many years the principal will last. There are no guarantees, of course, but generally the lower your withdrawal rate, the better the chances that your money will last throughout your retirement. But when the earnings are less than the amount that is taken out, you are dipping into your principal, so your money will not last for a long time.

If you start withdrawing a small amount from your portfolio, and adjust it for inflation, the chances are that your money will last longer whether you invest relatively conservatively or aggressively.

So to enjoy a decent retirement, you need to be responsible for your old age by starting to save adequately and invest prudently for your retirement as early as possible. I also believe that it is just as important that people take financial advice well in advance of their anticipated retirement. We have to carefully assess their investment portfolios, as this could make all the difference in the long run.

Singaporeans are intending to retire later, and those planning to stop working between the ages of 60 and 65 will double in the future. With increased longevity comes increased risk of potentially outliving one's retirement assets.

Another point to note is the unexpected 'life events' that may happen. No one can predict what lies ahead in their retirement journey. While we can determine when we want to retire and exercise to keep in good health, there are no certainties in life. Planning for one's retirement years must include taking into consideration life events that have the potential to disrupt your retirement years.

Hence, certain protection products – like medical, hospitalisation and long-term care insurance – are still needed during one's retirement to protect against the potentially devastating effects of unexpected life events like death and chronic illness. We need to have a financial strategy that is flexible enough to adapt to a person's changing needs and circumstances. Retirement can truly be great, but only if you carefully manage your money throughout your golden years.

05 Getting Down to the ABCs of Planning for Retirement
The Sunday Times, 27 October 2019

Among some things to consider are your future expenses, savings and sources of income, if any.

AFTER working in the financial sector for the past 30 years, it forces me to think about retirement now and then.

My framework for a comfortable retirement is to achieve three priorities – to have a roof over my head, be debt-free and have a regular income.

In most cases, if a person is prudent with his spending, he can achieve the first two easily. It is the third priority that is a challenge to many. How do you determine how much money you will need for retirement?

Most practitioners use the universal rule of 70 per cent of your last drawn salary as your retirement income.

Or some may use their current expenses as an initial guide and adjust the amount for their retirement lifestyle.

In both cases, you should include an estimate for inflation, since prices continue to creep upwards by at least 1 to 2 per cent in most years.

So, your desired income will be your starting point, and you will need to work backwards to calculate what you will need to have for retirement.

From there, calculate how much savings and investments you have currently and how much it will grow to upon retirement.

If there is a shortfall, you have to save more to plug the amount.

The next step is to calculate how much to save to produce the income you need.

Pre-retirement is all about accumulating while you are working, and that can be done through saving and investing. Post-retirement is about consumption all the way.

The truth is, individuals tend to get more conservative as they get older, so they become more cautious when investing for the future.

One way is to compromise on the amount of retirement income, which to some extent will help to reach a reasonable outcome. Of course, if your health permits, you may consider working for as long as you can.

When it comes to investing in a retirement plan, ensure that the payouts for your retirement are robust and personalised to your needs as you will be committing a significant portion of your life savings.

Once you know how much you need, you can determine how to generate that amount each month.

You can combine your retirement plan savings with other sources of retirement income, such as the annuity scheme Central Provident Fund (CPF) Life plan.

The bigger the amount in your Retirement Account (RA), the greater your monthly CPF Life payouts will be.

To build up your CPF Life account faster, you can do a voluntary contribution to your RA to the tune of $7,000 a year, and get tax relief at the same time, subject to conditions.

But remember, CPF Life monthly payouts only start from age 65. If you intend to retire earlier, you will not be able to count on your CPF Life payouts to tide you over.

You may also want to consider opening a Supplementary Retirement Scheme (SRS) account and use it for investments.

The SRS is a tax deferral scheme in which Singaporeans and permanent residents can contribute up to $15,300 a year and be eligible for tax relief.

SRS payouts start at age 62 (or the statutory retirement age when you make your first SRS contribution), which is a great stop-gap measure while waiting for your CPF Life payouts to start.

If you are using your SRS savings to invest in stocks, consider picking up some dividend-yielding ones, which can be a meaningful source of passive income once you have accumulated enough.

Stocks that pay dividends regularly are typically stable businesses such as retail real estate investment trusts (REITs) and telcos. They tend to be less sensitive to market cycles.

Some individuals look for an insurance company that offers a specified amount of income for as long as you live or within a specific period. However, you need to pay premiums for an agreed period in exchange for receiving an income during your retirement years.

Unlike the CPF Life scheme, which starts providing payouts only from age 65, and the SRS from age 62, individuals have the flexibility to choose when to start receiving their monthly payouts. This can be from as early as 55 to as late as your 70s.

You can also choose the premium terms that best fit your needs. There is an option for those who have substantial savings to pay a single premium.

For those who are nearing retirement, a shorter premium payment term of between three and five years may make sense.

In addition, many of these retirement savings plans offered by insurers also include a small insurance component, providing you with basic added protection.

Singapore Savings Bonds (SSBs) should also be considered. They are available in small portions and provide risk-free, short-term returns for the interim period when you have no immediate use for the cash.

They are issued by the Government and offer a risk-free investment to grow your retirement nest egg. This month's tranche offers an average return of 1.74 per cent a year over the entire 10-year holding period.

SSBs also provide liquidity, allowing you to withdraw your money if needed. You can also drop this investment at any point, without penalty, by giving just a month's notice.

This makes it attractive for anyone who wants to invest their excess funds or savings for future expenses during retirement but are not sure when they will need it.

At the same time, due to the increasing life expectancy of Singaporeans, many are running into the problem of outlasting their savings. Many retirees are worried about how long their money can last.

Finally, retirement does not mean you stop living a meaningful life. On the contrary, you can live your life pursuing your biggest passions and interests. To ensure this, you need to have sufficient funds for your retirement.

It is imperative you plan well in advance for this stage of your life.

Keep in mind that there is no single 'right' approach. It is important to stay flexible by adjusting your approach over time as your circumstances change.

06 Insurance in a Time of Uncertainty
The Sunday Times, 8 November 2009

Insurance is an excellent tool for wealth creation, yet some people believe that life insurance is a waste of money. But think about what will happen to your family if you were to die tomorrow. Will your family have sufficient money to maintain their standard of living when you are gone? That is why I extended my coverage to $1 million at the age of 47. I want my family to be provided for should anything happen to me.

EVERY year in July, I review my financial plan to check if I'm on track towards reaching my financial goals. As I was reviewing my life insurance coverage this year, I realised that today's environment is highly unpredictable compared to that of 10 years ago.

Today, my job requires me to travel around the region for at least a fortnight every month. Though air travel is generally safe, frequent travelling exposes me to an increased probability of a mishap. In addition, being in a foreign country means I am exposed to the threat of terrorism and unexpected occurrences.

My two teenage children are still in school and both will go on to tertiary education in a couple of years. Even though I have an education plan for them, a catastrophic event or another financial crisis could drain my assets and destroy the best of my investment plans.

Hence, I decided to bump up my insurance budget and expand my life insurance cover by an additional $1 million of term insurance for 15 years. This is in addition to the $1 million cover that I already have. My annual premiums amount to about $10,000 per year as the $2 million cover comes from both term and whole life plans.

The virtues of life insurance are obvious. By paying a premium to the insurer, I get to enjoy the coverage as it will step in to meet its obligations should anything untoward happen to me. Most importantly, I know that all my family's financial needs are well taken care of.

When I shared this with my friends, most of them commented that buying insurance at 47 years of age is just too late. Well, the life insurance industry has evolved over time and there are now more options available to people like me. In recent years, it has become increasingly popular for life insurance firms to launch new, innovative term insurance policies. In addition, they are more willing to accept larger sums insured. Previously, this was not the case.

Some of my friends also commented that the extra insurance premium I have to pay will reduce personal funds that might otherwise be available for additional investments. For example, if $3,300 is invested every year for 15 years, at an annual growth rate of 7 per cent, I could have accumulated $83,000.

However, I take an opposing view. By paying $3,300 a year, should premature death occur in those 15 years, my family will be better off with a guaranteed $1 million worth of death benefit. So there is a trade-off between putting off insurance and investing your money.

But let me be very clear about the role of insurance in personal financial planning. Insurance serves purely as a protection tool.

When an underwriter looks at your insurance proposal, your health condition is a major criterion to evaluate. My experience tells me that by the time you hit 45 years of age, or even earlier, some health symptoms may appear and will hinder your insurance application. For example, common health problems such as hypertension, diabetes and high cholesterol levels may cause the insurer to request a higher premium. In my case, my health has always been good, except for mild hypertension. If I were to wait till next year, who knows what will happen to my health.

The next factor is age. As we grow older, insurance premiums will naturally become more expensive, so I would want to buy insurance as soon as possible.

According to my calculation for a particular insurance product, the premium I would have to pay at age 47 would cost me $3,300 per year. If I wait till age 50, the premium will be 45 per cent higher. That's why it is important for you to increase your coverage when you are younger.

Some may ask why I bought a $1 million insurance for a 15-year term. Well, let's assume a person earns $100,000 per annum. In 10 years' time he will earn $1 million. Essentially, he is protecting 10 years of future income that would otherwise vanish if premature death occurs.

In 15 years' time, I will be 62 years old. By then, both of my children will be in their late 20s and should be financially independent.

Initially, I thought of adding a critical illness rider, which would increase my premium from $3,300 to $7,600. I chose not to do this because I already have $400,000 of critical illness cover from my existing policies and that should be sufficient.

> **Caution before you choose whole life insurance. Make sure you have the means to support your premiums after retirement.**

Some of my friends asked why I did not choose a whole life plan. Well, I would have to pay more for it compared to term insurance for the same $1 million coverage. I did not like the idea of paying more and having to carry on paying that sum even after retirement. My belief is this: before you choose whole life insurance, make sure you have the means to support your premiums after retirement.

When we choose insurance, we want it to be cost-effective, and we should select the coverage that helps protect our family's long-term financial interests. Determining which insurance coverage would be most beneficial to you requires:

- a knowledge of your needs;
- an appreciation for uncertainty;
- an understanding of the best product alternatives; and
- complete objectivity in the decision-making process.

These factors are important when you are considering buying insurance. If you do your homework, finding the right insurance won't be difficult.

Author's note: the financial strategy described in this article may not be suitable for all readers.

07 Life Insurance as a Wealth Planning Tool
The Sunday Times, 1 December 2019

"It is an asset class that can add value to any portfolio and meet life's changing needs."

IN the world of investing, diversification is a common terminology used to describe the process of allocating capital with the view of reducing exposure to a particular asset or risk.

When you invest in the financial market, you are exposed to systemic – the market risk – and unsystemic risk – the unique risk. So investment managers use diversification to reduce volatility by investing in various asset classes.

But diversifying your portfolio does not guarantee a positive performance or the ability to protect against losses. Hence, another strategy used by investment managers to protect against financial loss is to hedge against the risk using derivatives such as options, futures or forwards.

Similar to the concept of derivatives, the death benefit in life insurance is a hedge against the risk of a contingent or uncertain loss. So the main objective of buying life insurance has always been its death benefit, as it can act as a source of funds for debt repayment or income replacement at death.

Hence, most people perceive that the purpose of purchasing life insurance is mainly for risk management. To a greater extent it is true, replacing an individual's economic life value with liquidity (money) that can support any immediate financial needs, making life insurance an important part of wealth planning over your lifetime.

UNIQUE CHARACTERISTICS

Besides providing liquidity at death, there are other unique characteristics of life insurance compared with the other asset classes.

In today's complex world, it is even more important to incorporate life insurance into wealth planning to protect assets and ensure funds are properly transferred when the time comes.

The death benefit is paid in the event of the policyholder's death instead of a financial market event. That means the death benefit is largely insulated from the market's ups and downs. So no matter what happens, the death benefit is a guaranteed payout upon death, thus providing financial certainty at a predictable cost.

Another characteristic that makes life insurance a unique asset class is the death benefit payout, which is typically protected from a creditor or liability claim. The fact is, the transfer of assets from an insurance policy is passed by contract and not through a probate. Moreover, the contract of life insurance policy cannot be contested thus, ensuring that your beneficiaries can receive the death benefit in full.

In addition, life insurance provides potential cash value where the policyholder can withdraw or borrow against it, creating an avenue for retirement income, education funding, or whatever reasons you may need it for in the future.

Furthermore, life insurance helps to diversify your investment portfolio, especially when the financial benefits from the insurance policy are not correlated to traditional asset classes like equities or bonds.

When thinking of a portfolio of financial asset class, life insurance may not come to mind immediately, but it should. Often, investors may not realise that life insurance is also a very effective tool when it comes to diversification.

WEALTH TRANSFER AND ESTATE PLANNING

Think about it this way: Because of its uniqueness, the role of life insurance can extend into wealth transfer, estate planning and even for charitable purposes.

If you have a family business, you may have developed a succession plan to ensure a smooth transition of your business to the next phase, whether to sell it, pass it on to the next generation, or get external professional help to run it.

In scenarios like these, unforeseen circumstances like premature death before the handover of the business will trigger a liquidity event, which will have a negative impact on your succession plan.

Similarly, in many small businesses, it is the founder who holds the firm together and its success depends on him (the key man).

In a tragic situation, such as the premature death of the founder, there will be a detrimental effect on the continuity of the business. To prevent this from happening, key man insurance is a solution to help the firm survive the blow of losing the main person who makes it work.

The family members can use the insurance death benefit to sustain the business until an alternative solution is found. Thus, key man insurance gives the business some options to extend its life other than immediate bankruptcy.

That is why involving life insurance in a succession plan or business continuity planning is appropriate. Though the primary role of life insurance is to protect against the consequences of premature death, it is also a useful tool to create liquidity to keep your business running after you are gone.

Life insurance can also help you to divide your estate equally and fund the inheritance for your child who is not involved in the family business, which may help to prevent family squabbles.

In most cases, the fate of a family business is a challenging and emotional process. So you need to plan ahead to avoid potential conflict and to allow your firm to continue, to preserve family harmony and to thrive for generations to come.

For those with a philanthropic heart, life insurance can help to accomplish your goal by donating the death benefit to your favourite charity. Naming the charity of your choice as the beneficiary of your life insurance policy will provide a lasting legacy for a cause you believe in. This will allow you to gift into perpetuity.

Finally, given our longer lifespan, it may not be sufficient to implement financial plans that focus only on income accumulation through investment alone.

In today's complex world, it is even more important to incorporate life insurance into wealth planning to protect assets and ensure funds are properly transferred when the time comes. At the same time, to generate sufficient liquidity for the family, business and other financial needs at the time of death.

This is where life insurance can play a critical role in protecting your family and your legacy, and should be one of the pillars in planning for your financial future.

08 Beating Inflation at its Own Game
The Business Times, 30 January 2008

> As a student you learnt about the causes of inflation, but it did not really affect you until you started working and having a family. That was when you realised that inflation is a threat to your lifestyle and will affect your standard of living. But is there a way to mitigate inflation? Yes, there is. You can invest at least 15 per cent of your income, control your expenses and hold assets that act as hedges against price increases.

INFLATION is commonly taught in business classes as a situation where demand exceeds supply. For instance, office rents in Singapore have gone up because there is a lack of supply and an increase in demand. Students, though, might not be as concerned about inflation as their parents, who have to cope with rising bills.

Singaporeans today are feeling the impact of inflation on their standard of living. With oil prices breaching US$100 per barrel (in 2007), it is likely that inflation will continue to rise. The high price of oil is behind the rising cost of transport, electricity bills and food.

As a financial adviser, I find that clients these days inevitably bring up the topic of inflation. After listening to their laments, my advice to them is, first, take a deep breath and relax. However high inflation may be today, this is not the 1970s. (When the first oil crisis hit in late 1973 with a quadrupling of oil prices, Singapore's imported inflation surged. CPI inflation rose to nearly 30 per cent in the first half of 1974. At the same time, the global economy was headed for a slowdown. Singapore faced the prospect of stagflation — a combination of high inflation and low growth. This time round, the scenario is very much different.)

Before we discuss what an individual can do to lessen the impact of inflation, let's look at it from the macro-economic perspective. The central banks of Western countries, for example, the Bank of England and the US Federal Reserve, use interest rates as part of their monetary policy to control inflation. As inflation goes up, interest rates also rise to counter the inflation. Borrowers may be stretched servicing their loans as the interest rate rises. On the other hand, as base rates increase, the returns on savings should improve. Hence, people will borrow and spend less, and save more.

But Singapore's central bank, the Monetary Authority of Singapore (MAS), does not use interest rates to fight inflation; instead, it uses the strength of the Singapore dollar. The reason is that Singapore is a small and open economy that imports most of its food and fuel. With a strong Singapore dollar, we pay less when importing goods from overseas. So, Singapore's monetary policy is to maintain an appropriate level for the Singapore dollar with reference to a trade-weighted basket of currencies.

Singapore's interest rates are determined by supply and demand. The MAS does not directly control the movement of interest rates as these are independently set by financial institutions. This means that even if inflation is high, the savings rate does not necessarily move in tandem. That's why our savings rate remains low despite higher inflation.

Unfortunately, individuals have little control over inflation, which can creep up and diminish the value of savings over time. But don't fret. If you think about it, you have probably already hedged some of the higher costs without even realising it. According to the online research house Global Property Guide, Singapore's residential market was the world's hottest in 2007. It rose 24.3 per cent after adjusting for inflation (2.66 per cent), ahead of bullish markets like Shanghai and Bulgaria.

The majority of Singaporean households own their homes so even if you don't consider your house an investment, it has helped to hedge your family against rising prices. And while prices have gone up, earnings have also increased, in some cases, at a faster clip than inflation. If you happen to have skills that are in demand, you could command higher earnings. All this shows that the effects of inflation are being mitigated.

For lower income families and retirees, the government is offering help through the goods and services tax (GST) offset and other rebates. For essential items, NTUC FairPrice and other supermarkets are finding new sources of supply and offering house brands that can keep costs down.

However, the best way to mitigate inflation is to have a proper investment strategy. Investing in quality, blue chip stocks has traditionally been the best long-term way to beat inflation. The only problem is that if inflation becomes a major impediment to economic growth, the stock market will most likely suffer too.

One way to lessen that risk is to stick with big, blue chip companies which, by virtue of their size, have more pricing power than small companies. Moreover, because they have been beaten down and overlooked, large, blue chip stocks have the least room to fall should inflation threaten the equity market.

Another way to mitigate inflation is to consider investing in natural resources funds. While most people find it difficult to understand why gold prices have soared, it's easy to see why oil prices have shot up. Demand for oil is strong, and supplies are limited. The strength of the global economy, coupled with the difficulty in constructing new refineries, has led many market watchers to believe that energy prices will remain high for some time.

With a global boom in commodities — the staple ingredients of a modern economy — many experts see a fundamental shift in the market. For example, the price of wheat and soy beans rose 70 per cent in 2007, while prices of gold, silver, lead, uranium, cattle and cocoa are all at or near record levels. This is not a temporary situation, so any investment in this area will probably give you some hedge against inflation. All these strategies, however, call for proper asset allocation.

But if you think that the above is too complicated, consider this basic strategy. First, save and invest at least 15 per cent of your annual income. Second, control your expenses in any way possible. Third, buy and hold assets that historically have been hedges against inflation. Lastly, understand that inflation is difficult to quantify and that your personal experience will differ from others.

Ultimately, there is no substitute for awareness of the effects of inflation and being prepared to face it squarely. Individuals must also know the importance of inflation-beating assets and make them part of their overall portfolio.

> **The best way to mitigate inflation is to have a proper investment strategy. Investing in quality, blue chip stocks has traditionally been the best long-term way to beat inflation.**

09 Interest-Only Loans: the Pros and Cons
The Business Times, 14 November 2007

Normally, when you buy a property, you borrow from a financial institution and repay the loan through monthly installments. But do you know that there is another way where you pay interest only? So when do you use an interest-only loan? What are the advantages of using such loans?

CONSUMERS are constantly bombarded with offers of loans, overdrafts, credit cards and installment plans that promise instant gratification. We cannot avoid debt entirely, especially when it comes to acquiring the big ticket items, and not all debt is bad. But those who borrow must be prudent and know that they can make the repayments.

Even high net worth individuals (HNWIs) go to financial institutions for loans, which might seem strange since they are presumably cash-rich. But there are situations where it is worthwhile for HNWIs to borrow instead of paying with cash.

Some financial institutions offer interest-only loans targeted at the HNWIs. With such loans you only repay the interest, not the principal, so the loan balance remains unchanged. Most interest-only loans offered by financial institutions are associated with the purchase of property.

Interest-only loans make sense to individuals who are high income earners and in high tax brackets. The benefit comes from being able to save on tax on rental income. That's because the interest portion of loan installments for rental properties is tax deductible. This package also works well for short-term investors. By repaying only the interest, investors fork out less cash each month until they sell the property. As a result, they may be able to invest in two properties instead of one.

But interest-only loans are not for the long term because at the end of the loan period, the payment is raised to the fully amortising level. If you're still in your home at the end of the interest-only period, you'll have to start paying off the principal. The payments will be considerably larger because they will be amortised over a shorter period. For example, if your interest-only option lasts for five years and you have a 30-year loan, your principal payments will be calculated on a 25-year term.

There are drawbacks to interest-only mortgages:

- You could experience payment shock. As mentioned earlier, your monthly payment will go up — sometimes by 30 per cent or more — when you start paying off the principal. And if the end of your interest-only period coincides with an upward adjustment in your mortgage rate, you could face an even sharper hike in monthly payments.
- You are more vulnerable if your home value declines. Many borrowers with interest-only loans assume home price appreciation will help them build equity

in their homes. In recent years, that's been a good bet. But rising interest rates could deflate real estate values in some high-cost areas.

It's best to get a reputable financial institution to run the numbers for you and spell out the worst-case scenarios.

Equity provides a cushion against falling home values. Without it, you could find yourself owing more on your mortgage than your home is worth. If you sell, the proceeds won't cover your loan balance, which means you'll have to come up with money from another source. One way to avoid this problem is to make a good-sized downpayment on your mortgage.

The advantage of interest-only mortgages is that you have more flexibility. Some interest-only borrowers can afford a larger mortgage payment. However, their priority is to beef up their retirement nest egg or build up their emergency funds and once they've accomplished those goals, they often decide to increase their mortgage payments.

Increasing your monthly payments will build equity and lessen payment shock when you are required to start paying off the principal. If you are interested in this option, make sure your loan doesn't contain pre-payment penalties.

Interest-only mortgages are complicated, so make sure you understand the pitfalls before you sign anything. And don't rely on the financial institutions to figure out how much you can afford to borrow. A lender may not take into account all of your future expenses, such as your child's university fees or support of an elderly parent.

What worries me is Singaporeans taking two or more mortgages in a rising market. As property prices rise, the dollar amount also rises in line with higher selling prices. Affordability becomes an issue. You're in the best position to know what your financial obligations are, so get a mortgage you can afford.

How much should one borrow? There are two ratios that financial advisers commonly use. The first is the debt to asset ratio, which is total debt/total assets; this ratio should be 50 per cent or less. The second is the debt servicing ratio, which is total monthly loan repayment/monthly take-home pay; this ratio should be 35 per cent or less.

After all, wealth equals assets less debt. Wealth is built up over the years by accumulating assets and paying down debt, especially mortgage debt. When you pay down the balance of your mortgage, you are increasing your wealth by reducing debt. But an interest-only mortgage does not increase wealth in that way.

Of course, you may be increasing your wealth by accumulating assets instead. If that's your plan and you have determined that it is more effective in building wealth during the interest-only period than paying down mortgage debt, fine. But do note that paying down mortgage debt is the most effective way to build wealth, especially in today's financial environment.

Be wary of the four dangers related to borrowing too much:

- It can become a habit;
- It takes away money from other important needs;
- Your credit rating will be damaged if you don't pay the bills; and
- It can lead to high interest payments that are harder to make.

It's better to avoid borrowing when it comes to paying your everyday expenses or covering optional spending, and when you know you can't afford to service the re-payments.

It's also not a good idea to borrow a lot thinking that you will just pay the minimum back each month. It may take a long time to get out of debt and you'll end up paying a lot of interest. Also, if you have one late payment, your credit rating may suffer and you'll be charged penalties.

At the end of the day, paying down a loan is the best option because once it's paid, it remains paid.

❝During a bull run, any investor can look like an investment genius. While you may have been comfortable being a do-it-yourself investor when times were good, you may find yourself in a difficult position today. It may be time to consider finding a capable financial professional to help you.❞

❝To me, it is more important for HNWIs to keep the money they have than to accumulate more.... My advice is to think about security first, not growth. In today's bullish atmosphere, that might fall on deaf ears. But think about it this way: if you have several million in investible assets, you have reached a point where you already have enough.❞

10. A Pyramid Scheme that Works for You
The Business Times, 25 May 2000

> To be financially independent, you must put money to work early, and invest in a way that is suited to your goals.

ANSWER this: What is the biggest obstacle to saving for financial independence? If you say it's 'the high cost of living', 'I am not rich', 'inflation' or the 'crazy financial markets', you won't be alone. But you'd be wrong. Because, as difficult as these obstacles may seem, the one thing that can keep you or anyone from saving enough for financial independence is the challenge of money, time and growth.

To accumulate wealth you must put money to work, even if you only manage to put away a few dollars a month. Given time, these dollars will earn more than you realise. It is possible to build a sizable amount through savings small sums consistently and allowing time and growth to generate results. But first, you need, money however little. Without it, nothing can happen.

Time is an important element in financial planning. Money and time always work together. The more time we have the less we need to save each month to reach our financial goals. If you wait until you are in your 50s to save and invest you will need to put away at least 14 times more than someone who started savings in his 20s.

Money and the rate of return also work together. Getting rich through excessive returns is an idea that does not work. On the other hand, low returns that fail to keep up with inflation is just untenable.

So logically, we should put our money in an instrument that can earn more than average price increases. However, growth is related to our ability to accept risk. In the process of wealth accumulation, we need to invest in areas with reasonable growth rate, the faster it is to achieve our goals. But at the same time, the more likely is that we are exposed to higher risk.

Take for example in the table. If you want to accumulate $100,000, the amount of savings per month will depend on your time horizon and ability to take risks. The higher the growth rate the higher the risk level.

Monthly savings needed to reach goal of $100,000

Growth rates	5 years	10 years	20 years	30 years
3%	$1,547	$716	$305	$172
6%	$1,439	$615	$221	$100
9%	$1,338	$527	$157	$55
12%	$1,245	$451	$110	$29

Hopefully, by now, you can appreciate why early financial planning is so important. Financial planning was not heard of in the 1960s or 1970s. In those days, financial planning meant having as many children as possible. Hopefully, they would take care of their parents in their old age. But this traditional way is unlikely to work today.

So what is the meaning of financial independence? In my view, it can be defined as follows. You have a home that is fully paid and no other outstanding debts; sufficient cash in the bank and; assets that are producing a regular income. And of course good health is also as important. Once a person has attained all of the above he can be considered financially independent.

All of us need a roof over our heads. That home, regardless of whether it is private or public, must be fully paid by the time we retire. Many of us require loans to help us buy big-ticket items like a house or a car. However, please remember that debt is always a burden to our financial health. With debt, our cash flow will be diverted towards repayment, thus curtailing savings and investment opportunities. So the rule is to repay your mortgage and other loans as quickly as possible.

Establish an emergency fund first before investing. This even more crucial when we retire. As we age, we need to have sufficient liquidity to see us through any financial needs, like medical bills. In fact, saving for an emergency fund is the first step towards a secure financial plan. This account should be 'liquid' that is, it can be readily turned into cash. So even before thinking of investment, being with establishing an emergency fund as your first step. Having sufficient cash in the bank gives you extra money for unexpected expenses.

Then comes asset allocation. Your investment portfolio should reflect your investment goals and your risk comfort level. At the lowest risk level is cash, then bonds, unit trust and stocks, with futures and options at the top of the risk pyramid.

As we approach retirement we need some regular income to sustain our daily expenses. How do we create regular income? There are various instruments we can use. First, we have the mandatory minimum sum scheme in our CPF account. However, that alone is not enough. We can add on assets like annuity programmes, fixed income instruments or even an insurance endowment programme. Some financial experts recommend unit trusts, where you sell off the units that add up to your require income needs. Of course, this has a higher degree of uncertainty than annuities or fixed-income instruments. In any case, always bear in mind any tax liability that come with such programmes or instruments.

Imagine your financial planning as a pyramid. The base would comprise savings and insurance. The next level would be home ownership and a retirement plan. The third level would be investments and at the top, speculation.

If the pyramid is top-heavy, without solid support at the base, it can topple. For example, those who invest in commodities and options whey they have inadequate saving to take unnecessary chances and could lose everything.

All these components need to fit together like the pieces of a puzzle. The idea is to form a strategy that will give you peace of mind, protect you from life's little surprises, and allow you to retire comfortably. With your financial plan well in place you can rest easy.

I hope that you will be able to implement these strategies. They don't have to be done all at once. You can do a little at a time. Just make sure that you are consistent. Be determined. Be patient. Be Persistent. Your future depends on it.

❝To accumulate wealth you must put money to work, even if you only manage to put away a few dollars a month. Given time, these dollars will earn more than you realise. It is possible to build a sizable amount through savings small sums consistently and allowing time and growth to generate results. But first, you need money, however little. Without it, nothing can happen.❞

❝Conventional wisdom tells us that before thinking about investment you should have savings. Without savings there can be no investment, without investment there can be no accumulation. Most financial experts recommend that you put aside three to six months of your salary for an emergency fund. If you lose your job, it provides a financial buffer to tide you over the period without selling your investment, so your investment plan stays intact. Once this is established, you can invest the rest of your cash in other financial assets.❞

11 What Customers Really Want from their Financial Advisers?
The Sunday Times, 29 September 2019

Reliability, assurance and empathy among clients' top considerations.

CUSTOMERS who engage a financial advisory firm expect it to have a high standard of service, but that in turn requires a company to have an accurate insight into just what its customers want.

Customer satisfaction often depends on a range of factors, such as being treated with courtesy and respect, the staff having the ability to convey trust and confidence, and that transactions are handled efficiently and queries answered knowledgeably.

These factors are very much dependent on customer subjectivity, attitude and perception.

If an organisation does not have an accurate understanding of customer expectation during the pre-and post-sales service, then the chances of providing a high level of service are severely limited.

So it pays for financial advisory firms to be market-orientated and know accurately just what their customers expect.

TOP FACTORS THAT CUSTOMERS DESIRE IN FINANCIAL ADVISERS

Financial advisers were generally seen as being reliable, according to a poll of 204 people conducted here as part of my doctoral degree programme last year.

In fact, reliability was ranked the most important factor customers want in a financial advisory firm. These firms are there to help customers plan their financial future, so people expect an adviser to be reliable.

Assurance was ranked the second most important factor in service standards.

Desired qualities

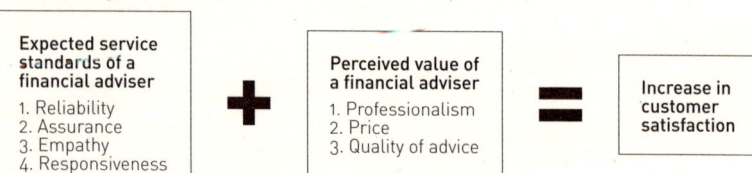

Expected service standards of a financial adviser
1. Reliability
2. Assurance
3. Empathy
4. Responsiveness

+

Perceived value of a financial adviser
1. Professionalism
2. Price
3. Quality of advice

=

Increase in customer satisfaction

When a higher level of service quality is extended to customers, customer satisfaction is achieved, if the financial adviser provides a higher level of perceived value, the customer will be even more satisfied.

Source: Ben Fok

This pertains to an adviser's knowledge, courtesy and ability to convey trust and confidence to customers. Advisers are expected to be attentive regardless of a customer's age and educational level.

So they should focus on improving 'soft skills' such as listening better and reading the body language of their customers in order to provide more accurate recommendations.

Empathy was ranked the third most important factor in the poll. Advisers are expected to provide personal attention, care and understanding to customers' needs.

This finding appears to reinforce suggestions that advisory firms must train their advisers in interpersonal skills, such as how to communicate better with customers.

The least important factor in service quality ranked in the poll was responsiveness, or the willingness of advisers to help customers and provide services.

While it ranked below other criteria, it remains essential with advisers expected to be willing to help customers and provide prompt services to meet their requirements.

The poll shows that responding quickly is one of the key drivers of service quality, so advisory firms must ensure that their employees are responsive towards customers' concerns and queries.

Given the role advisory firms have in planning for a person's financial future, it is expected that most customers prefer to have personalised services that can build a good long-term relationship. This would both gain trust and inspire customer satisfaction.

The poll also noted that customers have become particularly negative on the tangibles of financial advisory firms, such as luxury office renovations or the latest equipment.

This is an interesting anomaly and possibly due to the advancement in technology – innovations like robo-advisers, customised apps and other electronic means of doing business – making tangibles less relevant to customers.

Customers are, in fact, more concerned over the professional handling and care of their financial affairs by advisers rather than the sophistication or impressive ambience of the advisory firm.

CHOOSING A QUALIFIED FINANCIAL ADVISER

Three distinct terms were identified in the poll when it came to choosing an adviser.

The top criterion was professionalism. Singapore customers are comfortable working with financial advisers who possess professional qualifications, educational attainment and knowledge on financial matters.

It was also noted that adhering to a professional code of ethics is also highly important to customers, as it reflects an adviser's trustworthiness.

Customers also believe that financial advisers must continually undertake formal and professional training.

The price a customer pays was seen as the second most important criterion when choosing an adviser. The financial advisory industry is complicated in nature, so price includes not only fees but also commissions.

Consequently, the customer uses several criteria to determine how much he is willing to pay.

The poll suggests that transparency, value for money and suitability are of prime importance. Customers want to know the exact amount to outlay or the percentage of the compensation.

The poll also shows the quality of advice is the third most important criterion when choosing an adviser.

Customers who receive quality advice are more likely to trust the adviser more and to associate satisfaction with his or her services.

The quality of advice plays an important role in assisting an individual to plan for financial security. Customers also found that the financial advice they received was unbiased, was of a good standard, met regulatory obligations and, most importantly, met their expectations.

All this shows that if financial advisory firms are able to meet the expectations of their customers, they will create a trusting relationship and instil confidence.

Firms can improve service quality if they understand which factors to focus on and which to avoid. At the same time, they cannot focus only on one factor and ignore the rest.

These are critical issues when customers are considering engaging the services of a financial adviser.

Not only is it important for advisory firms to provide stellar service quality, but understanding customers' perception and expectations are also necessary.

Part 2

Learning from the investment world

Part 2 Learning from the investment world

THIS section will provide you with a better understanding of the world of investments. The investment universe is huge; you can invest directly in stocks, bonds, unit trusts and foreign exchange plus many others. How do you manage these investments? I will explain when you should be actively managing your investment portfolio and when passive management is appropriate.

I am also interested in how the wealthy invest their money. What do they do right in their investments that make them rich? Two articles in this section examine the investment traits of the wealthy and how they invest. There are certainly some very good investment habits that you can adopt.

A crucial component to investing is the Dow Jones Industrial Average (DJIA) which investors refer to everyday. But what is this average all about? What are the implications when the DJIA crosses a certain level? How will this impact your investments?

Do you also wonder why at times the economy looks real sluggish with high unemployment and poor macro-economic outlook, but yet the stock market rallies. How do you use that to your advantage?

Lastly, many financial experts use the term 'compound returns', but its meaning is often confused with a similar term called 'compound interest'. Do you know the difference between the two? The final article will explain in detail on the meaning of compounding while investing.

12 Getting the Most Out of Asset Allocation
The Business Times, 19 May 2000

Determine first your risk tolerance, then choose your asset classes.

FACED with choices for their savings and retirement plans, investors often pick one of two alternatives: the more aggressive, usually equities; or the more conservative, cash. This is because most investors are familiar with equities and cash, and not any other assets.

There is a price to pay for investing solely in equities when the market takes a turn for the worst. But investors who keep their assets in cash are equally hurt. The bank interest they earn merely beats inflation, or they may even have negative inflation-adjusted returns.

Let's not forget other assets such as bonds and tangible assets like the house you live in, jewellery and paintings. Unfortunately, most asset allocation practices do not add real estate to the equation. Only financial assets are considered. If this is the case, how can an investor know his appropriate asset mix? The best solution is to match the prospective rewards from each type of investment against your ability and willingness to bear risk. By allocating money into different asset classes like equities, bonds and cash, the investor is seeking to minimise risk while maximising return.

This is called asset allocation and it refers to the mix of investment vehicles in your portfolio. Research carried out in the early 1980s, called Brinson Study, showed that asset allocation accounted for 92 per cent of a diversified portfolio's returns. Security selection, or stock picking, was responsible for 6 per cent while market timing brought in only 2 per cent of the returns.

Any fund manager will attest that this is still true today. Again, this study involved only financial assets.

An investor must carefully consider three main factors before he determines his asset allocation. He must:

- have a solid understanding of the capital markets, their return and risk characteristics, and their historical relationships to each other;
- have a clear picture of his near-term and long-term liquidity needs; and
- determine his risk tolerance, or pain threshold.

Over time, stocks have been both the best performing asset class and also the most volatile. While stocks outperform other classes in the long term, they may provide negative returns during short-term periods. Bonds provide historically lower returns but offer a consistent cash flow and fairly predictable pattern of returns. Cash provides you with liquidity but the lowest returns. Therefore, a trade-off emerges between how much short-term risk or equity exposure one is willing to accept in order to provide added value over time. Some portfolios have longer time horizons and can afford more short-term fluctuations.

However, the investor must constantly balance short-term and long-term demands. If you engage a financial planner, he should work towards a long-term relationship with you, so he can re-evaluate your investment time horizon and risk tolerance, and make changes accordingly.

Perhaps the most crucial and most difficult factor in the asset allocation process is determining the pain threshold or risk profiles. Most planners will ask the following questions to determine your risk tolerance:

- How much risk is truly risky?
- How much risk can you afford to lose?
- How much in value swing can you take?

The next decision is to choose the asset class. Capital market theory suggests that the more asset classes a fund uses, the higher the probability that the fund will achieve an acceptable return for a desired level of risk.

A variety of asset classes can be used, each with its own characteristics and purposes. A fund can effectively control returns and volatility by diversifying amongst asset classes.

An investor can make informed future decisions and managers, asset allocation, and other investment factors once they have an accurate and thorough evaluation of a fund performance. We analyse the following aspects of a fund: strength and weaknesses of the fund's overall structure; the risk taken to achieve past returns; returns compared to other professionally managed portfolios of similar asset mix; manager's impact achieved through security section; and the impact of the manager's efforts to time the markets.

Like any other financial plan, your investment programme will need to be updated routinely as your needs, goals or risk tolerance changes.

Diversification underpins any investment portfolio. The aim is to offset one set of risk associates with one assets class against another. Hopefully, you come out the winner. Asset allocation is diversification in practice; it is also the most critical part of portfolio management.

Finally, there are no specific asset allocation guidelines that can be applied across-the-board to everyone. The reason is that the asset mix of person's investment portfolio is a function of many factors such as age, income, risk appetite and desired lifestyle. However, professional planners do work with general scenarios as a preliminary step, before fine-tuning them to meet investor's specific objective.

Tips on asset allocation
40 years to retirement

You've just started your first job. You can only afford to put aside modest sums of money, which can appreciate quite a bit over the years. Your portfolio should be weighted heavily on growth instruments and you should try to maximise returns with equity investment and with very little cash. Your most likely objective is to accumulate enough wealth to purchase a house.

25 years to retirement

You've more or less settled down, and are saving for the education of your children, if you have any. Your time horizon is mid to long-term. You're still in a position to seek high returns through equities. Your portfolio should still be more weighted towards growth as your need for an investment income at this point is still not critical.

15 years to retirement

You are now at your highest level of earning capability, and your saving level should also be at its highest. You can't afford a major financial setback. Increase the percentage of medium and low-risk instruments. Start thinking about creating regular income in 15 years' time.

5 years to retirement

Your children are grown up and you are near retirement. Your income level will diminish and so will your financial responsibilities. Your portfolio should put more emphasis on income and less on growth. Try to minimise risk and achieving a degree of regular income. Start thinking about how to preserve your capital that will last through your retirement years.

13 Building an Investment Portfolio for Life
The Business Times, 7 May 2004

Investment policy sets up a clear investment strategy to identify goals, review performance.

IF you want to build a good unit trust portfolio, you should start by hunting for top performance or better still, award winning funds, Right? Wrong. Too many investors set out to find such funds without setting up an investment strategy. To me, it is not a wealth building strategy as the chances that you will hold the right stock at the right time or the right fund are extremely low.

Conventional wisdom tells us that before thinking about investment you should have savings. Without savings there can be no investment, without investment there can be no accumulation. Most financial experts recommend that you put aside three to six months of monthly salary for emergency fund. If you were to lose your job, it provides a financial buffer to tide you over the period without selling your investment, so your investment plan stays intact. Once this is established, you can invest the rest of your cash in other financial assets.

A lot of planning has to go into the investment process. The first thing is to write down your investment policy. An investment policy statement provides the foundation of all your investment decisions to be made by an investor. It serves to identifies goals and create a systematic review process.

Investment policy is intended to keep investors focused on their objectives ignoring short-term swings in the market and provides a baseline to monitor investment performance of the overall portfolio and fund managers.

With the investment policy statement, the client can expect to have a clearer view whether or not their portfolios are achieving the stated goals and objectives. In addition, it provides for changes to the investment plan to be evaluated and the strategic policy reviewed. Hence, the investment policy statement has a realistic objective; secondly, it helps to define the asset allocation policy, and thirdly, it establishes management procedures. Lastly, it determines communication procedures.

Most people are also daunted by the numbers involved in formulating an investment plan. But you'll need to get used to the discipline of knowing your finances and quickly. As a matter of fact, the task can be quite liberating. You will be able to know exactly what you need to get to your objective, and be accountable to yourself along the way. There are online interactive calculators or adviser that can help you figure out your future money needs. The more specific you are, the more likely you will be to set and achieve reasonable goals.

After you have a rough idea of how much money you'll need and how much time you have to get there, you can start to think about the investment vehicles that might be right for you and what kind of returns you can reasonably expect.

Remember that you have your retirement plan and child's university education to consider. You must continue to save for tomorrow – even if you invest only small amount at a time. Generally speaking, an equity investment may be your best bet for the long haul because it has historically delivered higher returns over time.

Individuals who prefer to invest on their own can turn to many sources for investment advice- such as books, magazines, newspapers, unit trust companies, banks, stock brokers and websites. However, here are some pointers on planning for wealth accumulations:

- Retirement funds should be invested primarily in equities and long-term fixed-income securities. At the end of the day, when we retire we need to have assets that can provide us with a regular income. Investment in stocks should decline as an investor ages. This is a popular investment principle called Life Cycle investing. Wealthy and younger individuals can generally tolerate greater risk.
- All investors should diversify their total portfolios across asset classes, and the equity portion should be well-diversified across industries and companies.

If you are going to earn decent returns over time, you need to settle on an appropriate mix of asset classes. Make sure you diversify broadly, keep down investment cost and save regularly. Thereafter, it's a matter of sticking with it. Don't be swayed by market turmoil or over-hyped investment opportunities. You don't need to do anything extraordinary to get returns that will set you up well for later life. And finally, don't lose sight of your investment policy, which is the foundation for your investment plans.

14 Your Ticket to Investing Wisely
The Sunday Times, 22 February 2009

> Successful professional investors are like successful generals; they have realistic objectives and a clear strategy. So, to be a successful investor, you need to have sound investment strategies. But you first have to consider where you are now, where you want to go and how to get there. Using the analogy of a plane ride may help you achieve your financial goals.

OVER the last few months, I have counselled many investors who have lost money in their investments. Over time, I realised that all they really wanted to know were: What should I do now to get out of this mess? If the best time to invest is now then tell me, what should I invest in? Do I have to follow every piece of advice given? How do I identify advice that is good for me?

With the financial crisis hanging over our heads and no one knowing how long it will last, the best approach is to get back to basics. I would like to use the analogy of taking a plane. One of the things that airline crew are trained to do is to adhere to a standard operating procedure.

Similarly, an investor also needs to have a proper investment procedure.

The first step is to know where you are going and how to get there. In other words, you need to know your destination and how much time you need to reach it.

To most investors, the objective of investing is to make as much money as possible. That's fine, but how much and when do you need it? Without knowing your investment objectives, it's difficult to know what you should be investing in.

Most investors understand that investments span a range of risks. If you require a high return, you must be prepared to take a higher risk. Using the plane-ride analogy again, once the plane is airborne, you as a passenger have already exposed yourself to greater risk. Of course, the risk is mitigated by the fact that the pilot is well trained to fly the plane and to react to unexpected events.

Likewise, when investing, you should consult a financial adviser who takes the time to understand the risk level you can tolerate. Just as the pilot is trained to fly a plane, a financial adviser is trained to do the job of managing risk.

Your choice of investments must flow from your risk appetite. If you can take a 50 per cent drop in your investments, then high-risk investments like technology stocks/funds or aggressively managed funds like small-cap funds could suit you. If you cannot tolerate too much volatility, opt for lower-risk investments like balanced funds where there is an allocation of 60 per cent in equities and the rest in bonds, for instance.

The idea is to make your risk appetite — not the investment opportunity — the reference point. Most investment disasters happen when investors make the investment a reference point and then try to adjust their risk appetites accordingly.

Back to the analogy of the plane ride. When airborne, the plane may hit turbulence. For your safety, you are advised to return to your seat and put on your safety belt. But you will also notice that the turbulence usually doesn't last very long. Once the plane is out of an air pocket, it will be flying smoothly again.

The thing is, even pilots cannot tell the exact locations and severity of turbulence along their flight paths. All they can do is to build a good forecast by analysing charts, flight monitors and weather conditions. This is the reason they ask you to fasten your seat belt whenever you are seated, just in case the plane suddenly hits an air pocket.

To me, the current financial crisis is the turbulence in our investment horizon. Investors can expect the market to be volatile. The markets will eventually recover, but we just need to sit tight and ride out the market turbulence.

Finally, the plane reaches your destination and you will be glad that the risks you have taken are over. However, before landing, the crew will be busy checking landing procedures. This is akin to meeting your investment objectives.

The final phase of your investment horizon is extremely important. As you approach retirement, you should adjust your risk level and think about preserving your capital. Otherwise, you can have a hard landing like what many are experiencing today.

> Fasten your seat belt. To me, the current financial crisis is the turbulence in our investment horizon. Investors can expect the market to be volatile. The markets will eventually recover, but we just need to sit tight and ride out the market turbulence.

Once you step out of the airplane, you know that you have arrived safely. Similarly, in investing, you will arrive at some point in the future and hopefully fulfil your financial objectives.

The entire process is the result of knowing your investment objectives, taking some risks and enjoying the fruits of your labour.

15 Game for Stock Investing?
The Business Times Weekend, 21 February 2009

> Direct stock investing is not for everyone. You have to know yourself and whether you have the ability to invest in stocks. Moreover, there are many ways to invest. Apart from the simpler hands-off approach, there are many strategies that can suit different levels of interest. Understanding your personal investment preference is crucial to successful stock investing.

OVER the last three months, I was invited to speak at several conferences in the region on investing in the stock market. As we all know, the economic news is hardly encouraging, corporate earnings are horrible and the stock market remains volatile. Yet, investors at the conference somehow managed to look beyond the headlines and were still interested in investing in the stock market.

Not surprisingly, many in the audience understood that in a crisis like this there are opportunities. During the question-and-answer sessions, many wanted to know whether it was the right time to buy stocks; and if they were to buy, which stock they should buy, whether they could trade in this market, what they should do with their existing stocks, etc.

Well, I do not have a 'one size fits all' answer, but you need to understand what your investment objectives and strategies are. Telling me that you want to make money is not good enough; I need to know the type of investment strategy that suits your preferences. Understanding your own investment preferences is a crucial part of forging a sound investment strategy.

Nevertheless, before you start looking at the different stock investment strategies that are available, you should first know the answers to a couple of simple questions.

First of all, how interested are you in becoming more active in stock investing? If you are not interested, then a simpler hands-off approach would be preferred. For example, one of the most simple and effective hands-off methods of stock investing would be to invest in Exchange Traded Funds (ETF).

On the other hand, if you want to actively manage your stock investing and pursue higher returns, then there are many stock investment strategies that can be selected to best fit your level of interest.

Secondly, how much time do you have to manage your stock investments? Certain stock investment strategies require more time than others. A good stock investment strategy shouldn't take more than a few hours per month to implement. If you subscribe to a stock investment service, you can reduce that time because they take care of the most time consuming part of the process — the upfront research. The key is to find a good stock investment strategy that can help you to accomplish your goals and can be completed within your allocated time for investment.

Thirdly, are you investing for income or for growth in stock value? In general, you can classify stocks as income stocks or growth stocks.

- Income stocks produce a dividend during a specific time period such as every quarter, which provides income on a consistent basis.
- Growth stocks might produce a dividend, but are mainly purchased for growth in stock price.

Often if you want to be a stock picker, you need to follow some form of fundamental analysis. You need to believe that the stock market can incorrectly price its stocks, but eventually with time the correct price will be obtained. The focus is on finding these undervalued companies and purchasing their stock, and then selling the stock when the stock is fully valued or even over-valued.

Some people follow the buy-and-hold strategy; they are very selective in picking the companies to invest in and will hang on to the shares once they have them. This is how the majority of fund managers conduct their stock picks. No doubt, it is time consuming. You also need to know how to read financial statements and understand the economic cycle, and have an idea how the stock in question is performing and ultimately how it will affect your stock price.

This stock-picking method is for investors who believe that the world is a logical place and see investment analysis as a funnel. Stock pickers usually start with the economic outlook and then look where the business cycle is and what will happen to interest rates, currency inflation, unemployment, etc. Then they take a view on the industry, such as the industry cycle, profitability and competition, before conducting their financial analysis. Once this is done, they make or adjust their overall asset allocation accordingly.

Another strategy is market timing. Of course, getting in and out of the markets at the right time can pay handsomely. But this is a tall order. You need to have forecasting skills, and you need to use a number of mechanical systems to predict the market-turning points. To be successful, market timers need to have a good understanding of the broad picture of the economy. However, due to the lack of information, not many investors can do this successfully.

On the other hand, if you are thinking of trading the market, you need to understand technical analysis. This relies on charts and indicators that revolve around price and time, such as moving averages, volume and relative strength of stocks, just to name a few. There are way too many stock indicators to name them all here. Traders are out to make a quick buck by buying low and selling high. They do not mind what they are dealing in, and professional traders sometimes hold a stock for a remarkably short time. They resemble market timers but operate on a much shorter time horizon.

As you can see, each type of stock investment strategy analysis has its advantages and disadvantages. There is no clear winner as to which method is the best. It boils down to what you believe in more than the system. It's about what you feel is a valid reason to buy a stock. If you don't believe that a low PE (Price-Earnings) ratio is a strong enough reason to buy a stock, then you should not be using that type of investment strategy.

If you don't understand the investment strategies described above, there are alternatives available to you. However, while selecting individual stocks will take more time than just selecting a unit trust fund or an index, your efforts can be rewarded with greater returns. When you purchase a unit trust fund or an index, you are purchasing a large basket of stocks that have been pre-selected for you. It does make it easier to diversify, but there is a downside to this theory because some of the stocks might be going through a down period, which will reduce your overall return.

In any case, in times like these, it's more important than ever to have a focused investing strategy that suits you and which you should stick with. You can easily destroy your long-term returns by dumping stocks after the worst of a decline is already over and missing the rebound. And it's equally easy to hurt your returns by going bargain hunting too soon and being blindsided by a second wave of share price declines.

So think carefully about the gaps in your portfolio and wait for the right opportunity to fill them. At the moment, we are experiencing the stock market version of a perfect storm, where everything seems to be going wrong at the same time.

That always looks scary, but it also means that an awful lot of bad news is already reflected in share prices. Traders may have to worry about short-term market risks. But if you are investing for retirement or any other major financial goal that is a decade or more away, you've got a much easier job.

The key ways to minimise your investing risk are well known. You've heard them a hundred times before. Buy high-quality stocks and diversify as broadly as you can by owning shares of companies in a variety of industries.

What about those who already have a stock portfolio and are bleeding badly? Well, you have to reboot your portfolio and maybe sell off your dud investments. There are many cases where stocks that were traded at $5 have plummeted to $2.50 or even lower. There are those optimists who hold on to such stocks with the hope that they will regain their original values over time. But if the publicly-available information is telling you that there is something fundamentally wrong with the company, it may be best to off-load the stock at any price you can get.

Perhaps now is the best time to invest in large-cap (large market capitalisation) stocks. The simple truth is this: investing in large-cap stocks gives more certainty because these companies are able to sustain themselves better in a recession. While large-cap stocks are at times the quickest to fall in an impending recession, they are very sensitive, and when a market recovers, they tend to rise on the first wave of recovery.

Of course, investors dislike bear markets and view them with apprehension, especially those who don't have faith in economics and business cycles and are not confident about the future. The lack of such confidence makes it hard to stay the course. A natural temptation after watching the market or the value of one's portfolio decline is to think about 'getting out', moving to cash or hitting the 'panic sell' button. Don't get worked up by the fact that you have to cut your losses and do not compare your performances with others. Instead, link your performances to your preferred investment strategy.

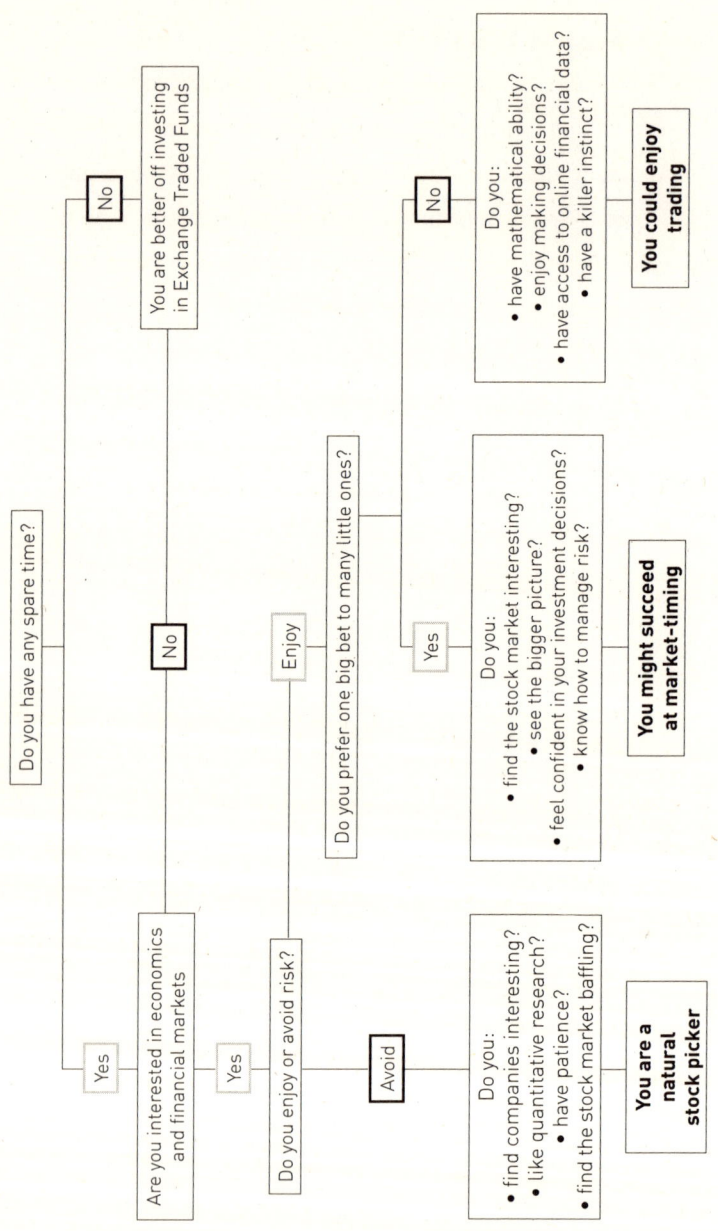

16 Invest Like the Rich and Your Returns May Be Better
The Sunday Times, 10 August 2008

Having been in the financial industry for over two decades, I have met many wealthy people who have since become my clients. I'm always fascinated by how the wealthy behave when they invest their money in the stock market. There are certainly some things we can learn from them.

TO the average investor, investing in stocks may seem more profitable and exciting than investing in unit trusts. Most people view the stock market as an effective way to meet their long-term investment goals. They place a major part of their savings in it and hope for a decent return over time. Sadly, not every investor understands what it really takes to be successful at stock trading.

Being a financial adviser with years of experience in dealing with the wealthy, I am always fascinated by how the wealthy invest their money — especially in stocks — and how they achieve successful money management.

With time, I've begun to understand that, unlike the average investor, the wealthy do not sink their wealth into stocks alone in their efforts to accumulate further wealth. More often than not, they have other investments, such as real estate, or they run a successful business.

In addition, when the wealthy invest, they usually do far more research than the average investor. They are interested in the type of business they are investing in, and will study the company's fundamentals, its business model and how unique that model is. Furthermore, they look into the company's long-term potential growth and, most importantly, they have a good understanding of how the business is being managed. Note that billionaire investor Warren Buffett has said that Berkshire Hathaway makes its money not from stock investing, but from actually acquiring and running companies over the long term.

When I conduct investment seminars, I always ask the participants to raise their hands if they have ever read an annual report or attended an annual general meeting (AGM) of the companies they have invested in. I am no longer surprised with the few hands I see. Few people bother to open up the reports or attend the AGMs.

Annual reports can seem intimidating and boring. However, if you want to know how the company's business is being run and the state of the business, you should take an active interest in the reports, and try to understand the balance sheet, profit and loss statement and other crucial financial statements. If you do not even bother to do this much, you deserve to lose money because there is no such thing as a free lunch. The more you read the annual reports, the more enlightened you become about the inner workings of your investments, which in turn makes you a more savvy investor.

The one rule followed by the wealthy is to invest based on fundamental stock valuation so as to buy at a low price. Actually, it is more than just low price — they want to buy it at a discount to the real value of the stock. This style of investing requires careful research and discipline. But it's a strategy that can produce high returns relative to risk, because when you do buy you are buying at 80 cents on the dollar, or even 50 cents.

Investors are often reminded by the stock market that the value of their shares can go up (the bull) as well as down (the bear) without warning. That is why people who try to time the market often do not beat it. As a result, they end up losing money again and again.

While the average investor thinks of short-term gains, the wealthy invest in the long-term prospects of the company. History has shown that over time, the stock market will recover and share prices will rise again. That is why Mr. Buffett's favourite holding period for stock is forever. To benefit from making good long-term investments, you must select your company stock carefully.

When I was a stock dealer in 1998 and during bear market corrections, I noticed that only the wealthy investors were buying. The average investor would try to determine how low the stocks would go and how long the corrections would last. Investors who added to their portfolios during downturns invariably benefited from higher market values during the next advance.

Wealthy investors understand that corrections are as much a part of the normal market cycle as rallies and they can be brought about by bad news or good news. The average investor always over-analyses when prices become weak and loses his common sense, but when prices are high, he buys. He ends up being the 'buy high, sell low' investor. When the majority of stocks are falling, wealthy investors see it as an opportunity; the average investor, however, sees it as a problem.

To be a successful investor, you need to research companies for their value. You need to focus on why you are including the stocks in your portfolio and accept the normal behaviour of your stocks in the face of different environmental conditions. You need to overcome your predilection for short-term investing and embrace a long-term approach that focuses on your portfolio objective.

For now, I advise you to relax. The current correction could well turn into an opportunity.

17 Investing Tricks of the Wealthy
The Business Times, 19 December 2007

> This is another observation on how the wealthy manage their money. It's interesting to learn how they grow and preserve their wealth; they know what they want their investments to achieve. You can also apply the same techniques to your own investments, regardless of how big or small the size of your portfolio.

RECENTLY, I asked a wealth manager whether an average investor can make more money by mimicking the investment strategies of the rich. His answer: not really.

Later he explained that the rich invest differently because, well, they're different. They can take more risks because they have more money to lose. Furthermore, they can speculate and have a short-term view because losing money is not a problem for them.

Well, I do not totally agree with his opinion. For the past few years, I have been advising wealthy people on their financial well-being. As a financial adviser, my job is to help these rich clients search for financial services that meet their needs. Through my interaction with them, I have gained some insights into how they accumulate wealth.

I can tell that the rich don't necessarily have any special insights into which stocks or assets are going to soar.

But what they do have is the confidence to apply a disciplined and systematic approach to managing their money. They have the habit of applying common sense to each investment opportunity facing them. Even though the interests of wealthy investors are not always necessarily aligned with those of the average investor, there are a number of principles and strategies employed by wealthy investors that do apply to virtually anyone who seeks to invest for the future.

It is a common fact that most financial textbooks teach us that in order to build wealth we need diversification, wealth preservation and strategic growth. To me, this not an accurate statement in itself because two of those strategies, diversification and preservation, don't help to build wealth. Perhaps the rich use these two strategies to maintain wealth.

After they have accumulated great wealth, the rich tend to preserve the wealth they have built. Average investors have not yet reached the ranks of the financially independent, so they are generally more concerned about investment growth and losses. The wealthy, as a general rule, do not have this concern. At the same time, they learn how to avoid taxes legally so that they can keep their money working for them. They also learn how to pass their assets on to their heirs without the government taking a huge part of what they have spent their lives building.

Another common perception is that the rich take more risk and therefore they accumulate wealth faster. However, the truth is that the majority of rich people do not build their fortunes by speculating on high-risk investments.

My experience tells me that the rich do not rely heavily on high-risk investment vehicles like hedge funds or venture capital funds, but are moderate risk takers who put more than half of their money into listed securities and keep a large amount as cash. This is because they have so much money that even if they do not meet their goals for investment growth, it would not be bad news to them; however losing their financial independence would be devastating.

So how do the rich invest? Unlike the average investor, the rich think long term in most of their investment strategies. They believe that there is power in long-term thinking and many of them make it habit of doing so. Great investors like Warren Buffett always invest for the long term. His investment successes include Washington Post Co, where Berkshire invested US$11 million in 1973; by the end of 2006, the investment was worth US$1.3 billion. That is 33 years of holding power — a clear demonstration of his investment philosophy. Most wealthy people do not engage in short-term speculation but have a long-term goal in mind.

However, the rich make use of risk by taking advantage of risk. They often build fortunes using volatile assets and investments, but that doesn't mean they are engaging in risky behaviour. They understand the risk and embrace risk because they know it always brings an opportunity for growth.

The average investor, on the other hand, is fearful of risk. Nevertheless, taking risk for the rich does not mean taking a shot in the dark. The rich take calculated risks — that means they gain knowledge first and consider the consequences of failing before taking action. The rich overcome fear with knowledge because knowledge can cause fear to fade away.

The rich also demand value for their money. Otherwise, how do you think they got to be rich in the first place? Value to them is buying assets at a discount to its intrinsic value. So for them the right time to buy is when there is weakness in the market. They buy when others are despondently selling, and they sell when others are greedily buying. This requires the greatest fortitude but it's a strategy that also reaps the greatest rewards. This bargain-hunting approach to buying value has enabled them to buy quality assets at reasonable prices. So they buy when there is bad news and they sell on good news. They invest because they understand that the weakness is only temporary and the stock price has already priced in the negative news, and it's time for them to hunt for bargains again.

If we look back at the Singapore stock market, there were many opportunities for investors to bargain hunt and buy on bad news, for instance, during the Asian financial crisis in 1997/98, the September 11 terrorist attack on the World Trade Center, New York, in 2001 and the SARS outbreak in 2003. The rich take advantage of such negative events to buy assets, whether in real estate or stocks and wherever value can be found. The average investor, on the other hand, will seek to sell and get out of a bear market fearing that the assets will fall further in value.

To the rich, probably now is the best time to sell and get out of the market, when all asset prices have gone up in value. Over the past years, we have had very good reports about our economic growth and all the good news is now factored into the stock price, so for the rich it is time to sell.

Another investing secret of the rich is that they approach investing like a business. They set up a business plan, establish annual targets, then analyse the results. Importantly, they have reasonable expectations. At the end of the day, what they want to achieve is to increase their net worth, not their income. The rich truly understand the meaning of working smart, not working hard; in other words, to focus on growing your net worth is working smart but working for an income is working hard. As their net worth grows, they do not increase their spending; instead they increase their investment. By repeating this over the years, once their net worth is built to a certain level, they are free to do what they want. Hence, to increase your net worth, you need patience, knowledge and wisdom.

The rich also do not willingly pay more for investment services simply because they find a particular adviser to be charming or knowledgeable. Nor do they chase after the hottest manager or the most publicised fund. Instead, they go shopping for the best combination of reasonable fees and consistently good performance. However, they will pay for advice from people who have specialised knowledge in a field they need to learn about. They don't believe in free advice as it can often be the most expensive advice.

As you can see, most investing secrets of the rich are nothing more than a combination of basic common sense and knowledge. The difference between the rich and the average investor is that the rich have the self-confidence to stick to the basics and to find out what they need to know. They don't get caught up in the theory of the week or the trend of the month. It's an approach that is easy to articulate but difficult to follow.

However, the average investor can learn important lessons from the wealthy, specifically the need to manage both risk and their own investment expectations. The failure to match expectations to the risk an investor is willing to take can result in frequent switching among investments, or even worse. Now the good news for the average investor is that you can apply many of the same techniques to your own investments, no matter how big or small your portfolio is.

18 Pitalls of Foreign Currency Investing
The Business Times, 23 April 2008

> Many people are attracted to the advertisements they see in the newspapers about making money from foreign exchange. These advertisements usually include testimonies of attractive returns within a short time frame. While this may be true and foreign currency investing may be lucrative, disruptions in financial markets and movements in exchange rates could result in financial loss. So is foreign currency investing for you?

WITH current interest rates for the Singapore dollar at a low, many investors are flocking to financial institutions that offer attractive rates for foreign currency deposits. A foreign currency account is an account maintained in another currency. In Singapore, foreign currency accounts are denominated in currencies other than the Singapore dollar.

At the moment, banks are promoting foreign currency accounts aggressively. We see this on most bank websites as well as in newspaper advertisements. It's no surprise therefore that over the past few months, when advising clients on their stock portfolio, they often asked me whether they should be putting their money in foreign currencies instead. Their argument was that they stood to benefit from the yield and the possibility of capital appreciation due to currency appreciation against the Singapore dollar. And should the currency movement move against them, they would hold on to the investment.

Understandably, given the negative economic outlook in stock markets around the world, some people perceive foreign currencies as safe and high yielding investments, with some foreign currency accounts paying more than 8 per cent interest per annum. However, before you invest in a foreign currency deposit, consider the following.

In the world of investment, there is no free lunch. Investing in foreign currencies has a risk-return trade-off — meaning, higher potential returns are associated with higher risk. Foreign exchange markets can be volatile. Currency positions held in these markets may involve actual losses. Investors incur currency risk due to the possibility of large exchange rate movements against the Singapore dollar. From time to time, significant events can occur that disrupt the normal operations of financial markets. Examples are failure of a major financial institution, war or a major political event. Movements in exchange rates could result in financial loss to holders of foreign currencies.

Consider the exchange rate for the New Zealand dollar/Singapore dollar. If you invested in June 2005 and held until June 2006, your exchange rate would have changed from about 1.14 to 0.96. In Singapore dollar terms, you would have lost over 15 per cent due to the depreciation of the New Zealand dollar against the Singapore dollar. Even with an interest rate yield of 8 per cent, you still would have made a loss. Of course, the flip side is that you also stand to gain from the New Zealand dollar's appreciation if you invest at the right time. However, it is almost impossible to pick the bottom and exit at the top. All in all, the crux of the issue is that foreign currency investing is risky and never a sure-win bet.

Then what about stocks? When you buy a stock, you are buying a piece of the issuing company. Admittedly, it's probably a small piece. But that share gives you the right to participate in the company's growth (or decline) and to vote on matters of some importance such as its directors, company auditors and some shifts in corporate policy. In some cases, you will also be entitled to dividends, whether as payments of cash or stock to shareholders.

When it comes to risk, investors can take some comfort in the fact that over very long periods, stocks have appreciated faster than the rate of inflation and have outperformed other traditional types of investments. That's because companies tend to grow with the economy and prosper and the shares in them allow stockholders to participate in that prosperity. Of course, none of this is any guarantee that you'll make money on the stocks you buy, or that being invested in stocks during a market downturn won't be plenty painful.

Since there's an art and a science to picking stocks and most investors would rather leave it to a trained professional to make those choices, unit trusts are a popular investment. Unit trusts are investment companies that pool the money of many people and invest it. The stocks or fund buys are determined by the fund's investment objectives — these are spelled out in the prospectus — and by the fund manager who makes the investment decisions.

So when you buy a piece of a stock/equity fund, you are actually buying an interest in all of the different stocks held by that fund. This gives you the benefit of diversification, reducing the risk that your stock portfolio will be savaged by a single bad stock. Although they are affected by the same forces that affect the market as a whole, many funds are managed to take advantage of upward trends or to protect investors against bear markets. For this reason, investors should rely on a well-diversified portfolio of equities and fixed income.

Don't get me wrong, I'm not totally against currency investment. In fact, a currency deposit can fit in as a minor part of the portfolio. It's just that you should refrain from investing a large proportion of your portfolio in currencies, because over the long term any movement of the foreign currency against the Singapore dollar may not be beneficial to the Singaporean investor.

Who should be suitable to open a foreign currency account? There are many good reasons for a person to put his money into a foreign currency account, such as hedging against exchange rate fluctuations for importers and exporters. If you open an account in the currency in which you make the bulk of your transactions, you can hedge against exchange rate changes by keeping money in the account until the currency rate is beneficial to you.

If you plan to send your children to study in a foreign country, such as Australia, saving for their education fund in an Australian dollar denominated foreign currency account will help you to worry less about the possibility of the Australian dollar appreciating. Individuals who are employed overseas or have regular income from abroad may also want to have a foreign currency account. For example, a non-resident working in Singapore may want to retain foreign currency salary received from his employer overseas.

Foreign currency accounts are suitable for those who have specific purposes such as those mentioned above. However, if you have a lot of cash and you have established a proper asset allocation in an equity and bond portfolio, foreign currency might be a good investment vehicle for you to diversify your portfolio. Read the terms and conditions very carefully; there are always some conditions attached to these investments.

Personally, at this moment, I'm not interested in a foreign currency account as the stock market offers plenty of opportunities to buy quality stocks.

19 It's Only a Number
The Business Times Weekend, 19 December 2009

> Investors are looking at the stock index daily to gauge the sentiment of the stock market. But what is so great about stock market indices? Does the 10,000 mark on the Dow have any tangible meaning for the economy, or is it just a symbolic number? And after we hit that certain benchmark, what happens next?

WHEN the Dow Jones Industrial Average (DJIA) broke 10,000 last month, it was telecast on financial news channels and traders were shown tossing commemorative caps, cheering, clapping and uncorking champagne.

The next day, several clients called me and made a big deal about this. Some suggested that it was time to accumulate and be aggressive. They interpreted the 10,000 mark as a sign that the economy was back on track and people were willing to invest again.

To many investors, passing the 10,000 mark is comforting. It feels like an achievement, especially for those who stayed in the market as the Dow plunged from its all-time high of 14,164.53 in early October 2007 to 6,547.05, taking their retirement funds down with it. The 10,000 mark is also a milestone of sorts — investments are roughly halfway back to where they started. So reaching 10,000 may help heal the trauma suffered by investors who watched the Dow sink. For them, it's more of a relief than a cause for celebration.

But what is the significance when an index crosses a threshold number? Does the 10,000 mark on the Dow have any tangible meaning for the economy, or is it just a symbolic number?

People, especially the Chinese, are often drawn to round numbers relating to various milestones in life. These include important birthdays or anniversaries. For many, 21 seems to be the first milestone of adulthood, 50 for reaching half a century, 80 for longevity and finally 100, the century mark, if you can make it. Each of these milestones is nothing more than an arbitrary line, which when crossed often encourages us to reflect on where we have been, what we have accomplished and, perhaps, what we should look forward to.

For the Dow, the relevant marker is often denominated by 1,000s — and 10,000 is significant to some investors. But frankly, this particular level does not have much economic impact or bearing. We know that as we approach these milestones, investors seem to anticipate them because trading activity increases. As investors become aware of a pending milestone, they may trade around the event, causing trading volume to surge.

This psychological influence is also apparent at the individual stock level. We do see more interest to round up prices from 0.49 cents to 0.50 cents or even from $1.99 to $2.00. As humans, we tend to be attracted to these numbers, which can create either resistance from above or support from below.

To me, the 10,000 mark on the Dow is a psychological event, not a key technical event. It merely means that the Dow's 30 stocks have combined to reach a certain level at which the aggregate average works out to 10,000. It does not mean that the economy is booming or about to boom. Nor does it mean that markets will continue to trend up. It's a number — that's all. But people feel excited about breaking thresholds.

Outside key psychological levels, there is nothing more to benchmark numbers. The real question is: after we hit these numbers, what happens next? Are there steady gains in gross domestic product (GDP) growth? Are macro-economic numbers looking better?

Remember, the Dow is a price-weighted index rather than a market cap-weighted index, which makes it not as representative of the overall market. Some investors reckon that the Dow lost its relevance decades ago. They say that in an economy as complex as the US, why bother with the ups and downs of just 30 publicly traded companies?

Nevertheless, we are used to monitoring the Dow closely — for some of us, even more closely than our blood pressure. We talk about the Dow at gatherings and in coffee joints. In the US, it remains the pulse-check of the economy.

Twenty years ago, when I first attended a course on technical analysis, one of the most important principles of the Dow Theory was that the movement of the DJIA and the Dow Jones Transportation Average (DJTA) should always be considered together. The two indices must confirm each other. That means that they must be moving in the same direction. When the performance of the indices diverges, it is alerting us to a larger fundamental problem and that a change to your investment portfolio may be imminent.

This technical rule is fundamentally logical. If the market is truly a barometer for future business conditions, in an expanding economy investors should be bidding up the prices of both the companies that produce goods and the companies that transport the goods. It is not possible to have a healthy economy where goods are being manufactured but not shipped to market.

Nevertheless, one major criticism of the Dow Theory is that many of its signals have proved to be lagging. However, while a deviation of the DJIA and DJTA may not necessarily indicate buying or selling points, you may want to consider altering the percentage of your equity exposure. Even Warren Buffett has admitted that rail data is his single favourite indicator to watch. Perhaps that is why he invested heavily in the railway stock Burlington Northern Santa Fe recently.

Some market analysts see the 10,000 mark on the Dow as an illusion, because there are still lingering threats to an economic recovery — rising unemployment, weak consumer spending and a battered housing market. Also, we should not forget an asset bubble in Asia and the large US budget deficit amid a fragile economic recovery.

On the other hand, many analysts say that 10,000 can have psychological implications. Psychology plays a huge role in investing, especially during periods of panic and fear.

With more people all over the world investing some of their life savings in US stocks, the answer matters a lot. Many of us either directly or indirectly hold US stocks through unit trusts and other investment platforms, and some small investors are increasingly trading stock themselves over the Internet. It was reported that Singapore was the third top investor on Wall Street during the past quarter.

Closer to home, over the past 10 months, the Straits Times Index (STI) has almost doubled from its March low of about 1,500. At the time of writing, the STI stand at 2,790 — around halfway between the March trough and its historical peak of 3,831 in October 2007. Analysts are now more bullish about the general economy and expect the STI to cross the symbolic 3,000 mark very soon.

In conclusion, reading and studying the Dow gives us an indication of overall movement in the market and the future of the economy. When Dow crossed 10,000 for the first time, it was on 29 March 1999 — a time when the nation was enjoying an era of record level prosperity. Today, the crossing of the same 10,000 mark is telling us that things are better than they were last year amid a struggling economy. Hopefully, we aren't falling off that cliff as we move forward to yet another round number — the year 2010.

20 Making Sense of the Recent Market Rally
The Business Times Weekend, 15 August 2009

> The economy looked really weak during the first six months of 2009 with high unemployment, poor corporate results and a negative macro-economic outlook. Yet the stock market rallied. Do you know why? How do you stay in the game? One important reason for the bullishness is that the market has already discounted much of the bad news six to nine months ahead of time. What can you do in such cases?

RECENTLY, one of my clients told me he was confused about the significance of the recent market rally. Many of the blue chips, such as Singapore Airlines, NOL, SGX and CapitaLand, are still making quarterly losses. On top of that, some 47 companies listed on the Singapore Exchange have announced quarterly results with combined earnings lower than the previous quarter.

On the job front, unemployment is still rising. According to the manpower ministry, the worst is not over yet. This is the first time employment has contracted for two consecutive quarters since the 2003 economic downturn.

In addition, Singapore's gross domestic product (GDP) for 2009 is expected to contract by 4 per cent to 6 per cent. "Aren't all these bad news for the stock market?" he asked.

On the other hand, over the last four months, equities have done extremely well with the Dow Jones Industrial Average up 20 per cent; the Standard & Poor's (S&P) 500, 23 per cent; and the Straits Times Index (STI), 56 per cent.

The Singapore property market has also picked up with queues forming outside some new show flats. Housing and Development Board (HDB) resale flat prices have surged to a record high which has prompted the minister for national development to caution that speculation is creeping back into the market.

What is going on? Why is the stock market going up when the economy is still struggling? Who are the people buying these homes in a recession? Is this the start of an economic recovery and is the worst behind us?

Singapore's latest export data support indications that we are recovering from its deepest recession to date. Non-oil domestic exports (NODX) fell 11 per cent in June from a year ago, compared with a 12.3 per cent decline in May. At times like this, even a slight rebound makes things look better than they are, not forgetting that the Singapore economy is expected to grow only 3.5 per cent in 2010. So why is the stock market looking bullish despite weak economic data?

The answer comes from legendary fund manager Mark Mobius and billionaire investor Warren Buffett. Both of them believe that the stock market is a leading indicator of the state of the economy. In other words, it predicts what the economy will look like in six to nine months.

I'm no economist, but I'll share a few of my observations. The unemployment rate may be high, but it is a lagging indicator of economic activity. From past recessions, unemployment keeps rising even after an economic turnaround begins.

Singapore's GDP fell hard in the first quarter of 2009 and was followed by large numbers of layoffs. Neither of these statistics is good news. They suggest that deflation could be on the horizon. Deflation, or falling prices during a recession, is a troubling sign and could lengthen the recession, but this does not seem to be happening.

On the property front, Singaporeans' keen interest in property doesn't fade even in a recession. Currently, there is plenty of liquidity and mortgage rates are relatively low, and so, many are looking to buy property to take advantage of the low interest rate environment. There have been reports that the private property market is well supported by HDB upgraders who only need to pay a little more to upgrade as HDB resale prices are also rising.

One important reason for the bullishness is that the market has already discounted much of the bad news. Major indexes fell more than 40 per cent last year. But this doesn't mean the market will ignore all bad news. Unexpected news can still take the market lower. Currently, the market is responding to what the economic landscape is expected to look like in six months time. As such, I believe there is a good chance that the market is beginning a bottom-building process.

Keeping in mind that the stock market looks ahead by six to nine months, the revelations of the past year have long been digested by the market. This was also true during the Asian financial crisis when the STI fell to a low of 800 points in mid-1998. It was all doom and gloom and a few months later Singapore was in a technical recession, coupled with massive job losses and poor corporate earnings.

Stock market behaviour can be a sign of things to come, particularly the economy. The question here is whether we believe that the fundamentals have improved enough to merit a 9,000 in the Dow Jones, or a 900 in the S&P 500 or even a 2,600 on the STI. In other words, are stocks fully valued at this time?

For a sustained rally, there has to be growth in real earnings or positive earning surprises, improving home sales, higher employment — proof that inflation will not be a major problem down the road. Until positive data becomes consistent, we can expect the markets to start and stop, and go up and down with an upward bias. If the data worsens, then stocks will once again retrace their downward spiral, maybe even hitting previous lows.

In my 20 years of practice, most successful investors I know tend to focus not so much on today. What is expected to happen tomorrow is more important. In the short term, the market is unpredictable and subject to great volatility. But in the very long term, the stock market has had a strong upward bias. I don't know of any reason to think that this would change.

This is a key point that's easily overlooked in many investors' frantic search for the direction and the 'right' answers that they hope will yield instant gratification.

Personally, I believe that brighter days are ahead and that, someday, most of us will look back on the past two years as a very painful period that we managed to get through. Getting to that future won't be easy, but it will be a lot easier for people who can keep their heads when others seem to be losing theirs.

> ... most successful investors I know tend to focus not so much on today. What is expected to happen tomorrow is more important. In the short term, the market is unpredictable and subject to great volatility. But in the very long term, the stock market has had a strong upward bias.

21 Compounding the Issue
The Business Times Weekend, 21 March 2009

> When investing, whether in stocks or even fixed deposits, you will hear the term 'compounding'. Often investors understand the term 'compounding in fixed deposits' but not the term 'compound returns'. This article will explain the difference between the two. It is also important know how to apply this understanding to your own investments.

LAST month, I had discussion with a disgruntled investor about his investment portfolio. He claimed the concept of compounding in investments in stocks and unit trusts is completely flawed. His argument was that in compounding, interest is not only earned on a principal sum, but also on any accumulated interest. With that understanding, he concluded that with compounding, you should not lose money. So if an investment has the potential of losing money, then it is incorrect to apply the concept of compounding in investment!

To the people in the financial industry and also in academia, one of the most central and powerful concepts in finance and investment is the effect of compounding. Yes, this is often mentioned: 'rates of return' that are said to be 'compounded' over a time period with multiple intervals. This can often mislead investors who don't understand how money is made and lost over a period of time, due to compounding, in markets that move up in one year and down in the next.

I believe the confusion arises because some people fail to distinguish 'compound interest' from 'compound returns'. Compound interest comes in only when we are dealing with interest-bearing investments. Compound returns, on the other hand, apply to investments where a negative return is possible.

By its very nature, an investment return is subject to two factors that can drastically skew it. The first is dispersion of returns, and the second is effect of negative returns.

Before we move on, let's recall that 'simple return' is the average of a set of numbers while compound return is a geometric mean, which provides the cumulative effect of a series of returns. Moreover, the compound return is the mathematical calculation describing the volatility of an asset to generate earnings or losses.

For example, assume you had invested $10,000 in the Straits Times Index (STI) in 1988. The average annual return between 1988 and 2008 for the STI is 5.56 per cent. Using the annual average of 5.56 per cent, an investor would conclude that $10,000 invested in 1988 would become $29,511.25 at the end of 2008 — applying the concept of compounding $10,000 annually at 5.56 per cent for the 20 years.

However, at the beginning of 1988, the STI was 833.6 and it ended at 1,761.56 in 2008. This resulted in a compound average of only 3.81 per cent. In the stock market, you only get compound returns, so $10,000 invested at the beginning of 1988 in the STI would result in only $21,132 by the end of 2008 — ignoring the impact of dividends, transaction costs and taxes.

[Mathematical calculation using a financial calculator: annual average return from 833.60 to 1,761.56 = 111.32 per cent divided by 20 years = 5.56 per cent per year; Compound returns: PV = -10,000; FV = 21,132; n = 20; compute I = 3.81 per cent] The difference in the simple average return and the compound return is due to the two factors mentioned earlier — the dispersion of returns around the average of 5.56 per cent and the impact of negative returns on compounding.

The dispersion of returns is simply the average difference in returns as compared to actual returns over any period. Simply put, it is the set of returns that shows how far each year's returns has moved away from the average. Often, as the returns become more dispersed from the average, the compound return declines. Hence, the greater the volatility of returns, the lower the compound returns.

It will be helpful to demonstrate this by using an example. Look at the four portfolios in the table opposite to see how the dispersion of returns and negative returns skew the compound rate. Take note that the simple average return for all the portfolios is 8 per cent. Now let's see how portfolios with the same simple average return can have very different compounded returns. Clearly, the compound average return declines as the dispersion of returns widens.

Table 1 Rate of returns
The impact of dispersion and negative returns on four portfolios

Start with $10,000	Matthew		Mark		John		Peter	
Year 1	8%	$10,800	1%	$10,100	30%	$13,000	50%	$15,000
Year 2	8%	$11,664	13%	$11,413	24%	$16,120	24%	$18,600
Year 3	8%	$12,597	10%	$12,554	-30%	$11,284	-50%	$9,300
Simple average	8%		8%		8%		8%	
Standard deviation	0%		6.24%		33.04%		51.88%	
Compound average return	8%		7.87%		4.11%		-2.39%	

Mark's portfolio is the least affected as the dispersion is small. However, Peter's portfolio has the widest dispersion in returns compared to Mark's and John's. Therefore, Peter's portfolio compound return has declined the most, even as the simple average remains the same.

Finally, Peter's portfolio experienced a huge loss in Year 3 and the compound average return becomes negative. However, what is important for Peter is the percentage return required to break even after the loss. As the loss increases, the return required to break even grows significantly as a result of the negative effect of compounding.

A measurement of dispersion is the standard deviation, which tells us how volatile the returns are in the portfolio. The higher the standard deviation, the higher the volatility or risk.

In the table, Mark's portfolio has the lowest standard deviation of 6.24 per cent while Peter's has the highest, 51.88 per cent, making the latter the most risky of the lot. Needless to say, Matthew's portfolio is riskless as the standard deviation is zero.

So, we see that a wide dispersion of returns and negative returns would be detrimental to a portfolio. What can we do to mitigate the negative impact of compounding? We can start by minimising losses and/or capturing some profit from an investment. Another way is to rebalance your portfolio more frequently. Selling part or all of the top performers in one asset class or sector provides capital to invest in new promising opportunities. A variation of this strategy is to sell part of your position when you have a quick gain to capture some profit and move the stop to or above your entry price. In every case, the investor is actively seeking to offset the negative impact of compounding.

Another thought is that your stocks and funds generate income from dividends and distributions. When you keep that income in your account, reinvested in purchases of additional shares of stocks or funds, your earnings generate additional earnings and you reap the rewards of compound returns. Of course, compound returns do not assure an overall profit or positive return in an investment account, as stocks and reinvested dividends are subject to market fluctuation and changing economic conditions.

As you can see, compounding also works in your investment account, but when you introduce the possibility for the capital to be depleted by negative returns, compounding is no longer relevant. You can see how returns are relative to the time frame in which they are measured and the dispersion of returns. But more importantly, losing on your original capital can create a dent too big for a windfall return to overcome. If your portfolio value can drop, it defeats the purpose of compounding. So, if you understand how to address the negative impact of compounding, it can be a very satisfying experience. After all, it's your money that's at stake.

> Compound returns do not assure an overall profit or positive return in an investment account, as stocks and reinvested dividends are subject to market fluctuation and changing economic conditions.

❝Wealthy investors understand that [market] corrections are as much a part of the normal market cycle as rallies, and they can be brought about by bad news or good news. The average investor always over-analyses when prices become weak and loses his common sense.❞

❝So how do the rich invest? Unlike the average investor, the rich think long-term ... most rich do not engage in short-term speculation but have a long-term goal in mind. [They] make use of risk by taking advantage of risk. They understand the risk and embrace risk.❞

❝The ... rich ... have the self-confidence to stick to the basics and to find out what they need to know. They don't get caught up in the theory of the week or the trend of the month. It's an approach that is easy to articulate but difficult to follow.

However, the average investor can learn important lessons from the wealthy, specifically the need to manage both risk and their own investment expectations. The good news is that you can apply many of the same techniques to your own investments, no matter how big or small your portfolio is.❞

22 Low Cost for Pure Risk
The Business Times, 24 October 2001

What exactly are Exchange Traded Funds?
What are their advantages and drawbacks?
And who should invest in them?

THERE are two bugbears for investors in unit trusts. The first is the high upfront fee and the second is the forward pricing of units which means the price is unknown at the time of buying or selling.

Exchange Traded Funds (ETFs) address both concerns. They made their appearance in May, with five currently trading on the Singapore Exchange. They are Diamonds (tracking the Dow Jones Industrial Average); IS US Tech (Dow Jones US Technology Sector); IS MSCI Singapore (MSCI Singapore Index); IS S&P 500 (S&P 500) and SPDRS (S&P Depositary Receipts).

Recently, the Central Provident Fund announced that members would be allowed to use their CPF funds to buy ETFs, also known as tracker funds. A list of such approved funds would be made known at a later stage.

What exactly are ETFs? At the most basic level, they are baskets of securities that are traded, like individual stocks, on an exchange. They usually mirror an underlying index, making them akin to index funds. Most ETFs adopt the full replication approach, investing in every stock in the index, weighted proportionately. Since they are listed on the stock exchange, there is only the brokerage to pay (the same rate charged for stocks), against a typical 5 per cent front-end load for a unit trust. Most also charge lower annual expenses than even the least costly unit trusts, since ETFs are passively managed. Their second advantage is that the price is known throughout the day, and buying and selling can be executed immediately. In fact, ETFs can even be bought on margin. In short, anything you can do with a stock, you can do with an ETF.

Although ETFs are more flexible than unit trusts in many respects, their shares cannot be bought from or sold back to the fund company like regular unit trusts. The holder of an ETF will have to find a buyer on the open market. Furthermore, unlike unit trusts, ETFs do not necessarily trade at the net asset values of their underlying holdings. Instead, the market price of an ETF is determined by supply and demand. To a large extent, this is driven by the underlying value of their portfolios, but other factors can affect their market price.

In the US, heavily traded issues such as SPDRs and QQQs (which track the Nasdaq 100) generally trade close to the value of their underlying securities, but premiums and discounts do arise, especially for thinly traded funds. If an ETF trades at a discount to its net asset value, institutional investors can arbitrage by buying large blocks of the ETF, and redeeming them for the underlying shares which can be sold at a profit. The arbitrage opportunity should close the gap between their market price and the ETF's net asset value.

ETF risks

Despite their advantages, ETFs may not be for everyone. They may be riskier than actively managed unit trusts. ETFs, like index funds, give investors unprotected risk, i.e., the full market risk. In fact, by investing in a passive fund you are participating fully in bull and bear markets. The best return an investor can hope to get is the market average.

In contrast, in an actively managed fund the portfolio manager makes a buy or sell decision using various techniques. He picks stocks with good fundamentals and sells them when they are overvalued. By doing this, he is managing the portfolio actively with the aim of beating the market or an index. For this, the manager is paid a higher management fee. In most cases, an ETF stays fully invested at all times. Some actively managed funds may keep a portion in cash, more in the face of a bear market. For example, during the Asian crisis, most active fund managers sold stock to hold cash. This prevented the value of the portfolio from deteriorating. During that period, most active unit trusts had a cash holding of more than 20 per cent of the portfolio, against a normal level of under 5 per cent.

In comparing the index unit trusts and ETFs, each investment offers some attractive characteristics. ETFs provide significant trading flexibility. As listed securities on the stock exchange, they are easily traded and allow for leveraged positions using margin accounts. But traders incur significant transaction costs, which also limit the ETFs' attractiveness for smaller investors who invest a small dollar amount over time.

Significant questions also remain. The arbitrage process that keeps ETF prices in line with asset values has only been tested in the US during bull markets. Internationally, large discounts from NAV have been observed in times of market turmoil. How will the ETF arbitrage process function in a protracted bear market? Will institutional investors and market makers continue to step in to create and redeem shares?

Currently, the primary ETF investor is an institutional investor or market maker using ETFs to take a low-cost position in a sector or country. High net worth investors taking larger positions also find segment or sector ETFs attractive ways to generate exposure. Individual investors looking for technology exposure may find the Nasdaq-100 (QQQ) an attractive way to fine-tune their tech exposure.

Judicious mix

Finally, there is the question of where the financial adviser fits in with ETFs. The total cost structure of ETFs does not appear to create many opportunities for their passively investing clients.

For those thinking of investing in ETFs, study all the angles carefully before proceeding. The cost advantage of an ETF isn't always as large as it might seem, since trading costs can quickly add up. There is little doubt that ETFs do well in rising markets, but actively managed funds tend to pull ahead in volatile or falling markets. So don't put all your money into ETFs – have a judicious mix between actively managed and passively managed funds.

23 Index or Managed?
The Business Times, 28 September 2000

Understanding efficient markets theory can help you make that decision.

FOR many years, Singapore investors were investing in actively managed funds. Until recently, for the first time in Singapore, we had index funds that were being launched and now investors have a choice whether to invest in managed funds or index funds. Do investors really understand the reasons for investing in index funds? How do you decide whether to go for managed funds or index funds? By understanding the concept of efficient market, you would be better off in making that decision.

Let's define what an efficient market is. The theory argues that the prices of all securities quickly and fully reflect all available information about the assets. If so, then investors are unable to earn abnormal profits using that information.

The implications of an efficient market mean that an investor cannot consistently earn abnormal profits because the prices of securities adjust instantaneously to fully reflect all relevant information. "Consistently" is defined as by anything other than by chance and "abnormal profits" is defined as a return greater than a risk adjusted return.

So how can a market be efficient? We need:

- a large number of well-informed investors/analysts who continually evaluate the available information, and
- large, well-functioning security markets with significant competition between participants, resulting in securities being fairly and accurately priced.

Once we understand the concept of efficient market; we next need to understand the difference between index and managed funds – also called passive and active funds, respectively.

As the name suggests, passive indicates that the fund is unmanaged. This means that the fund manager will not make buy and sell decisions in the portfolio. All he does is to follow an index very closely. He will only change his holdings when there is a change in the index that he is replicating. Since index funds adopt a buy and hold strategy and don't have a manager to manage the portfolio, their fees are comparatively low. Furthermore, index funds have lower fees and may suffer less from market downturns then actively managed funds.

So by investing in an index fund, the best return investors can hope to get is the market average. Come to think of it, that's the worst they can expect to do, too. And that's the nub of the issue. Given the choice, would you want your manager to beat the index?

By investing in an index fund you are participating fully in a bull and a bear market. There is no need to outperform a benchmark. You are basically implying that fund managers are of little help in beating a benchmark. And on top of that you are happy with market returns. In other words, you believe that fund managers cannot beat the market and your view is that the market is efficient.

In contrast, in an actively managed fund, the portfolio managers make a buy or sell decision using fundamentals and technical analysis. He will buy a stock when fundamentals are good and sell when he thinks the stock is overvalued. He has to pick stocks with good fundamentals and sell those with a poor outlook. By doing this, he is managing the portfolio actively and his objective is to beat the market or an index. So for this he is paid higher management fee. And obviously, the cost of running such a fund is also higher.

Investors who invest in actively managed funds believe that the market is not efficient. As such, they believe that by actively managing the portfolio they can outperform the market.

Whatever category you fall into, here are some points to keep in mind.

Index funds provide the greatest probability that you will end up with your desired account balance at retirement, based on your asset allocation model. You probably won't have much less than you planned, and you may not have much more. This is because most financial planning models calculate your saving and investing schedule based on the performance of indexes.

With actively managed funds, managers sometimes stray from what the fund is supposed to be investing in (it's 'style'), in an effort to beat the benchmark. This can throw you off your investment track.

Beware of an index fund with high fees. Since index funds need little intervention in managing the portfolio, the fees should not be high, as high fees will erode your returns. Over time, very few actively managed funds outperform, index funds. This is because of the higher fees and the 'return to the mean phenomenon'. (An actively managed fund that is performing better than the index will move towards the index, as it will attract more assets.)

Index funds are representative of the stock or bond indexes that managers are trying to beat (the benchmark). Index funds cannot beat the benchmark because they are the benchmark. Similarly, they cannot fall below the benchmark.

Actively managed funds can, and probably will, do both over time. So if you prefer less fluctuation in your investments compared to actively managed funds, an index fund could be a good idea. Index funds do fluctuate, but only as much as the market does.

However, this does not mean that you should invest only in index funds. Well-run actively managed funds can give your returns a boost, especially if you have a long time to go before you retire. But you might still want to consider keeping some core holdings in index funds if you are a strong believer in the efficient market theory.

See diagram below

Are index funds for you?

Steps to tell if you are an efficient market believer

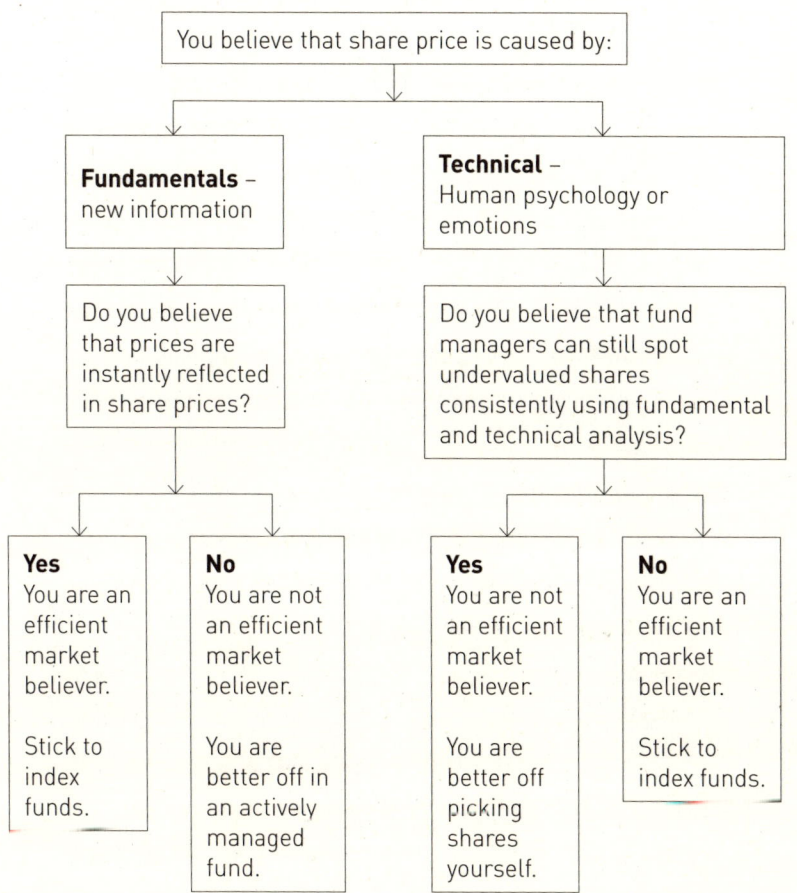

24 Bonds: Go It Alone or Go with a Fund?
The Business Times, 6 December 2000

> Diversification offered in bond funds is protection against risk, albeit at the expense of income.

WITH equity markets likely to finish the year with negative returns, individual investors and seasoned fund managers alike are turning wary. In fact, some fund managers are shifting their assets allocation from equities to bonds – the so called flight-to-quality.

Until recently, Singapore investors had little opportunity to invest in bonds. With issues by statutory boards like Jurong Town Corporation and Housing and Developing Board, retail investors can now invest in bonds with as little as $10,000. Previously, they would have had to turn to bond funds as a convenient and affordable way to invest in bonds.

However, there are important distinctions between bonds and bond funds that can be overlooked. Below, we examine key issues.

Many investors buy individual bonds because they offer fixed interest rate and are relatively stable compared with equities. Individual bond promise to pay a fixed interest rate (usually semi-annually) and return the face value (principal) of the bond at maturity. However, if a bond is sold prior to maturity, its market value would depend on the level of interest rate at that point in time.

Once a bond is issued and interest rates go down, the bond is considered more valuable (and will sell for more than the investor paid for it) because it is paying a higher rate of interest than investors could earn in the current bond market. If interest rates go up, that bond is considered less valuable as it is paying less than what investors could earn in the market.

This is referred to as interest rate risk, and only applies if a bond is sold prior to maturity.

Like the value of an individual bond, the unit price of a bond fund also fluctuates with interest rate changes, and when sold, could be worth more or less than its original cost. The unit price (known as net asset value or NAV) is simply the market value of all the bonds in a fund (less its liabilities) divided by the number of shares outstanding. NAV is recalculated on each business day to reflect the current prices of all the bonds in the fund.

Creditworthiness or default risk is a key factor in assessing the value and risk of bonds. Rating agencies like Moody's and Standard & Poor's play an important role in this process. The highest rating for a bond is AAA, with little likelihood of default. Bonds rated below BBB are non-investment grade.

A high credit rating usually has low yield while a poor rating has high yield. Here, risk and return go hand in hand. But beware, a rating above BBB is no guarantee against default. A classic example: The Government of Singapore Investment Corporation (GIC) was one of the biggest investors in China's Guangdong International Trust and Investment

Corp (Gitic) which collapsed in 1988 with debts of around US$3 billion (S$5 billion). At that time Gitic carried an investment grade rating of Baa2 by Moody's, which had deemed Gitic an acceptable credit risk.

So, even GIC cannot eliminate the possibility of loss in its investments (much less the individual investors), but it minimises its overall risk by diversifying its portfolio and holding different asset classes in different countries.

How can an individual investor diversify his portfolio with limited resources? By investing in a bond fund. Because a bond fund consists of a pool of individual securities, investors can purchase shares representing ownership of all the bonds in the portfolio, thus investing in a spread of bonds with far less money. And being diversified, a bond fund offers enhanced protection against risk.

Before an individual invests a bond instrument, he needs to know if he needs regular income. The higher the need for certainty of an income, the lower the tolerance for volatility. Individual bonds which pay a regular income may be suitable for retirees, for example. Bond funds do not distribute income as they usually reinvest it for further growth.

Another big difference is that a bond fund never matures. This is because a fund holds numerous bonds in its portfolio that mature at varying dates, so you cannot "lock in" an interest rate or the return of your principal investment. The maturity of a bond fund is stated as an average of all the maturities of the bonds in the portfolio and will fluctuate based on the bonds held.

A bond fund's average maturity can be maintained at a certain level, similar to a single bond, or adjusted based on the investment manager's assessment of interest rate trends. This adjustment in average maturity is accomplished by buying and selling bonds of either longer or shorter maturity than the portfolio average. This may result in greater level of realised capital gains and losses that if the fund held all securities until maturity.

Then there is macroeconomics. Where inflation is a threat, a rise in short-term interest rates is likely. One of the tools used by the US Federal Reserve Board to pre-empt inflation is to raise interest rates. By doing this, it slows growth in the economy, hopefully towards a soft landing. But if interest rates continue to rise to fight stubborn inflation, a hard landing may result with recession setting in. Therefore, inflation and interest rates go in the same direction. Bonds thrive in a recession because of the low interest rate environment. Equities suffer as companies' bottom lines will be hit. So fund managers will switch from equities to bonds in a flight to quality.

For investors, bonds withstand the test of time by providing long-term stability, a cushion against stock market volatility and a steady income component. As an alternative to individual bonds, however, a bond fund offers greater diversification, professional management and liquidity.

See diagram below

The bonds dilemma

Shall I invest in bonds?

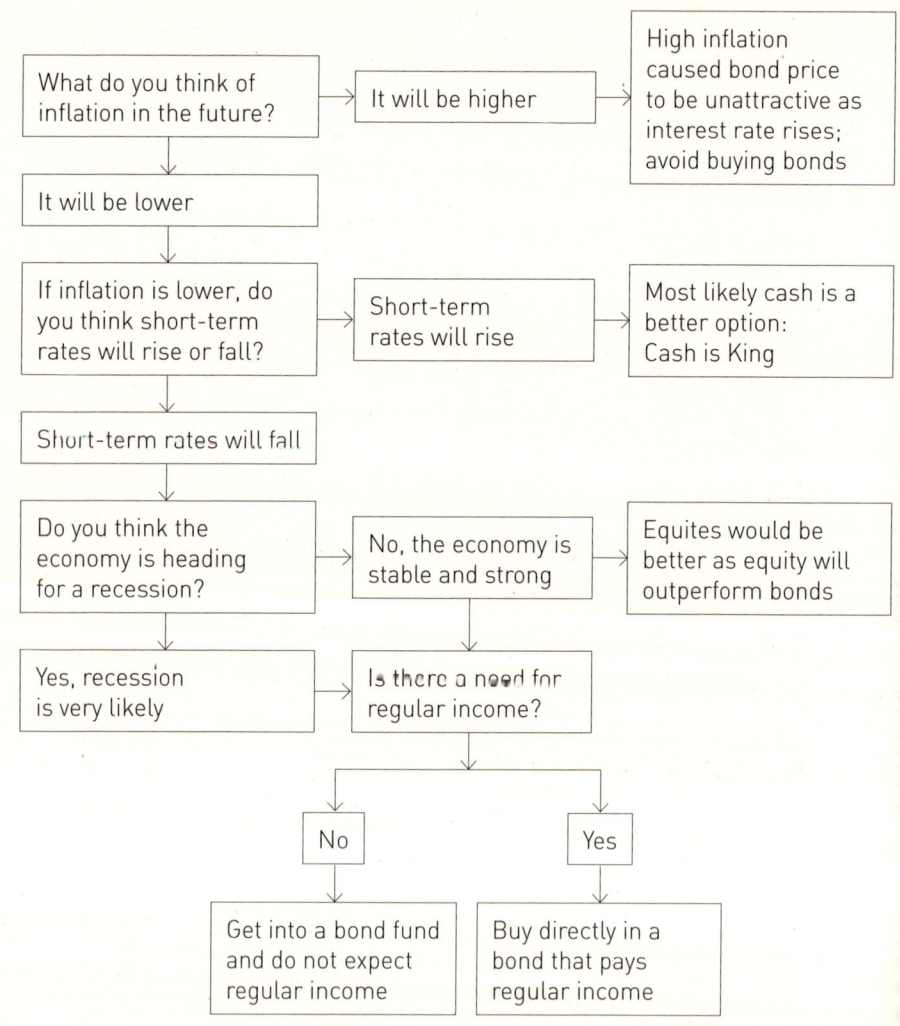

❝In an actively managed fund, the portfolio manager makes a buy or sell decision using various techniques. He picks stocks with good fundamentals and sells them when they are overvalued. By doing this, he is managing the portfolio actively with the aim of beating the market or an index. For this, the manager is paid a higher management fee.❞

❝Many investors buy individual bonds because they offer fixed interest rate and are relatively stable compared with equities. Individual bonds promise to pay a fixed interest rate (usually semi-annually) and return the face value (principal) of the bond at maturity. However, if a bond is sold prior to maturity, its market value would depend on the level of interest rate at that point in time.❞

Part 3

Understanding investment fundamentals

THE articles in this last section will provide you with an understanding of the strategies used in the investment world. In order to invest successfully, you need to understand the many issues and uncertainties that come with investing. It's only with a proper understanding of investment theories that you will be able to invest with confidence.

The fundamentals of successful investing are many, and include diversification, asset allocation, dollar-cost averaging and re-balancing. But what do all these concepts mean to your portfolio and how do you apply them to your portfolio? When you are faced with a global meltdown and your investment value shrinks every day, do you immediately change your investment strategy or have the faith to hold on? While sticking to tried and tested methods of investing can sometimes be boring, they may still work well especially in a bearish market.

In a depressed market when every stock is down, do you buy more stocks or sell more? How do you turn a bear market to your advantage? Do you focus on the losses or the opportunities that are available? Finally, do you know that you can shock-proof your investment portfolio in the event of a bear market?

These are simple investment principles, but they are difficult to execute. The following articles will provide you with an insight to good investment strategies and financial success.

25 GDP and Shares Prices: What's the Connection?
The Business Times Weekend, 28 August 2010

> The stock market is often a sentiment indicator that impacts Gross Domestic Product (GDP) either negatively or positively. Do you know how a bull market or bear market affects GDP?

LAST month I was discussing with Alex, on the strong gross domestic product (GDP) numbers that economists have forecast for the year 2010. Thanks to the strong manufacturing numbers and the optimism in the economy, the 10 economists who participated in the survey are revising their GDP number upwards. Some are forecasting GDP growth of as high as 13 per cent this year. Even if we take an average opinion of the 10 forecasts it is still a strong double digit growth of 11 per cent.

No doubt our economy has recovered very strongly. The Minister of Trade and Industry (MTI) reported that the economy expanded by 18.1 per cent in the first half 2010 from a year ago, unprecedented going by data from 1975. Furthermore, the MTI kept its full-year growth forecast at between 13 per cent and 15 per cent for 2010 which will be the fastest annual pace on record, if such growth figures are realised.

To add on to the good news, this solid recovery was broad-based with non-oil exports increasing, visitor arrivals rose about 20 per cent. Labour is thus extremely tight, this was evident from job seekers rejecting jobs offered by employers.

In addition, our property index is looking extremely robust. This has prompted the government to release more lands to meet demand. Both the private and public housing indices have climbed back to their previous peak if not higher. Another report also shows that the mortgage growth rate has surged 21 per cent year on year, demonstrating the confidence of home buyers. All these are signs pointing to a strong economic recovery and stock investors should be glad.

Alex was extremely happy with the performance of his portfolio, started in June 2009. He was doing extremely well. The Straits Times Index (STI) surged from 2,380.07 in June 2009 to 2,897.62 in December 2009, a return of 22 per cent in six months. This boosted his confidence and he began to increase his exposure aggressively in January 2010. But to his dismay at the end of June 2010, the STI was back to where he started. With the strong economic numbers why did the stock market not appreciate in the first half of 2010?

Indeed, the STI started this year at 2,897.62 and ended the half year at 2,835.51. Alex was perplexed.

Why is the stock market not performing? One reason is that Singapore is a small and open economy. We depend on external demand such as exports, tourism, and foreign investment for our growth. While Singapore is recovering strongly from the crisis, it is affected by what is happening around the world. Let us use the major indices as the barometer. The Dow Jones Industrial Average (DJIA), has fallen 7 per cent from this year's high in April amid the concern that European nation will struggle to reduce their budget deficits and speculation that the US economic recovery may be flagging. Technical analyst who are using the Elliot Wave theory warn that the DJIA and S&P 500 are displaying a bearish should head formation in the long term and intermediate term charts when breached there will be sell-off targets for most fund managers. Even Warren Buffet said the US economy is only 40 per cent to 50 per cent recovered after a wrenching ordeal last year.

At the time of writing, except for Thailand and Indonesia, the rest of the Asian stock markets are in the doldrums. The Shanghai Index has fallen 27.5 per cent this year as the RMB is revalued. There are also concerns over excessive asset price increases in Asia. All these factors can weigh down the stock market.

Exactly a year ago, I wrote an article in *The Business Times* in August 15, 2009, called 'Making sense of the recent market rally' explaining why stocks rose while the whole economy seems to be struggling. There I explained that the stock market discounts anticipated economic conditions. So the stock market rose in mid-2009 in anticipating of a strong economic growth in 2010. This was evident in our GDP growth in the first six months of 2010.

Thus looking at the STI, it would appear that the stock market is saying that it expects the economy to improve this year but is unsure about next year. What this means is that investors believe that corporations will post earnings rises this year. Since stock prices have risen so far, now is a good time to get out and re-assess the market.

Most investors believe that 'stock market up' is positive for the economy, and 'stock market down' is negative for the economy, which will impact confidence. As confidence shifts in correlation with the market, it will impact the willingness of both consumers and companies to spend and invest, and therefore impact future economic growth.

So the argument that higher stock prices presages faster economic growth makes a lot of sense. Since stock prices are the present discounted value of the future stream of expected dividend, an increase in anticipated economic activities and hence earnings and dividends should be associated with a boost in the stock market.

Investors should be aware that stock market prices and GDP measures two separate values. The stock market is a measure of how investor value individual companies with GDP gauges economic growth and contraction. Furthermore, the stock market trades on Mondays through Fridays, but GDP is reported on a quarterly basis.

This is not to say there is no connection between economic growth and the stock market. The prosperity of companies and shareholder depends on the health of the economy at any point in time, but instead of GDP growth predicting stock return, it is the stock market that predicts future GDP growth.

So the stock market and the economy do not move in tandem. Equity prices have a tendency to drop when the economy is in or about to fall into a recession. Yet similar drops occur in the stock market at other times as well. Frequently, the stock market precedes the economy in a recovery. This makes sense because stock investor are generally more concerned about the future than they are about the present.

Simply put, while short-run changes in GDP growth can affect stock prices, there is no long-term connection. Economic growth is determined by growth in the supply of labour and increase in productivity. Stock returns, on the other hand, are determined partly by the cost of capital which is the rate of return required by investors to bear the risk of owning stocks. In other words, it is primarily risk that determines long-term stock returns, or the returns on any investment asset and not the growth rate of the economy.

Avoid investing based on current economic performance alone. If this year closes as the consensus expects, we will end with strong GDP growth of 13 per cent to 15 per cent. This is unlikely to be repeated next year and then the stock market is expected to remain muted. Some economists have started downgrading GDP numbers for next year, as strong expansion this year has led to 'high base' effect for next year. This underscores the importance of having a globally diversified portfolio with exposure to many different countries, regions and asset classes.

26 Rein in Your Emotions
The Business Times, 17 October 2003

> Don't let impatience, fear of failure or envy cloud your judgement. Find a good investment strategy and be disciplined about it.

OFTEN, investors think they have the right strategy when the market rises after their share purchase and the wrong one if the market falls. But to be a successful investor, we must understand what to do and how to do it right.

While you understand that your success in investment depends on asset allocation, market timing, etc, you must also look at your own investing psychology. Hence, instead of focusing on what you already know, let's look at some of the psychological facets of investing.

Although I believe in asset allocation and market timing, I am equally interested in what it takes for somebody to be a successful long-term investor. In my opinion, how a person invests is like his driving a car. When we learn to drive, a good driving school will teach you how to drive and show you some defensive driving techniques. For example, if you know what to look out for on the expressways, it greatly improves your chances to reach your destination safely.

On your guard

Likewise, I think a good investment strategy should include techniques about defensive investing. If you know the pitfalls, you can guard against some of the obstacles that most investors do not see. For example, when you are caught in traffic jams, try to observe how impatient drivers behave. They look at their own lane and how the other traffic lanes are doing. It is always the case that traffic in the other lane looks like it is moving faster. Then you've guessed it correctly: they will swerve in and out to cut in front of someone else whenever there is an opportunity. Impatient drivers do this repeatedly, making use of any opportunity they can find to gain a slight advantage. These drivers may indeed gain a few seconds ahead of you. But in the process, they expose themselves to higher levels of danger and raise the blood pressure of other drivers.

In investment, it is like taking unnecessary risks for a small return. We have heard many times that patience is the foundation for successful long-term investing, and this applies equally to many investment strategies, whether it is strategies like buy-and-hold or market timing. Yet many impatient investors watch the market every day waiting for the opportunity to change lanes. By doing so, they do not give their investment strategy enough time to perform. Selling off too quickly (thus making small gains) is often the biggest mistake in impatient investors. I prefer to build wealth in slower lanes. Investors who stick to their long-term strategy may not have exciting stories to tell but are more likely to retire with more wealth and able to sleep better at night.

Over time, whether you like it or not, you would have developed a unique driving style. The style refers to the amount of dangerous driving habits you can and are willing to tolerate. So if other drivers do not behave the way you expect them to, you lose your patience. The difficulty is that you cannot control other drivers' driving habits.

In investment there are also risks that you cannot control, for example, market risk. So you must ask yourself, "Can I tolerate the risks involved in the asset class?" Let me recount an experience with a client: although the portfolio made money, he was unhappy because it was underperforming the benchmark. However, he forgot that two years ago, the strategy was to split his investment assets into four equal categories: domestic equities, domestic bonds, international equities and, international bonds. I recalled that after much discussion he understood what we were doing with the portfolio, but I could not help wondering what he was expecting. With only 50 per cent of his assets invested in equities, he could not have expected the portfolio to mirror the equity index.

And, in fact, one reason we set up his account the way we did was to make sure that it did not match the equity index. To this client, it felt as if he was missing out on all the action. His reaction was similar to your turning on the car radio when caught in a very bad traffic jam, and getting angry when you hear that several other alternative routes are wide open. It is an understandable reaction, but not very rational and not very helpful.

One track mind

Many investors also focus on hope while ignoring risks. While managing risks is at the heart of successful investing, you will almost never find an investment adviser who wants you to focus on risks. All they want is to focus on returns. All investors want to talk about is how much money they can make but not how much they can lose. But the correct strategy is to take care of the downside and the upside will take care of itself.

Another observation is that investors with relatively small amounts of money tend to take too much risk, while those who are flush take too little risk. It is like drivers who drive small cars tend to speed more than those with big cars.

At one extreme, people who have few assets feel they have little to lose and often spend their money on lottery tickets, thinking that it is their only ticket to financial success. Some of them think they are "investing ", when they are, in fact, gambling against overwhelming odds. In a recent article it was reported that with the economic slump, Singaporean spent $6 billion on gambling last year. That is a lot of money to lose.

On the other hand, many investors are too risk averse, especially those with 20 or more years before retirement. Most of their money is in bank deposits or sitting in their CPF accounts. I am not saying that bank deposits or CPF interest is a bad thing but the return is just too low. These investors are likely to realise, probably too late, that they have short changed themselves, forfeiting the retirement they could have in order to gain illusive short-term security. And they will have squandered their greatest asset – time.

Investing in equities has its risk but that risk can be controlled and can be small compared to the gains you are likely to give up by avoiding the equities markets. If you want to avoid big market losses you must sometimes sell your holdings, even when that means you have to take a loss. This is one of the hardest things for investors to do. Many people think that if they don't sell at a loss, they don't really have the loss. And they think that taking a loss, even for strategic reasons, means they are failures. As a result, people hang on to the loss-making stocks, often with the attitude that they will wait until they can break even, then sell and be done with it.

One of the best things you can do in investing is spend some time understanding your expectations. Of course, you would like a piece of the action when things are going well, and if you follow a sound investment plan you will get some of the action. But you will not get it all the time and you probably will not get it right away.

If you are not careful, your emotions can distort your perception, which can lead you to unnecessary conclusions and make it easier for an investment adviser to re-invest your money to suit his purposes – not yours.

Do you expect to never have a down quarter or a down year in the stock market? Do you expect never to have to suffer a loss and always make a gain? Think you will always like what the numbers tell you at any given moment?

Emotional control

In every case, you're setting yourself up for an upset. Some people are so competitive by nature that they cannot stand to see others doing better than they do. Other people are rarely satisfied with anything, always looking over their shoulder, asking why they could not be doing better. These people are bound to be disappointed. And if they do not have a disciplined approach to investing, their emotional reactions will start dictating their investment moves.

You can bet the professional in the investment business understand these psychological hurdles, and many of them are willing and eager to take advantage of investors who do not. When it is your money at stake, you should be the one in the driver's seat, even if you take directions from someone else.

The best way to keep your hands on the wheel is to have a plan that will work for you, and then stick to it. Do that by understanding the difference between your financial needs and your emotional needs. A good investment plan will help you achieve the total return you need to meet your own financial goals.

Happy investing.

27 About those Eggs ...
The Business Times, 14 January 2000

> Remember that old adage about eggs in a basket? Diversification is still relevant and for the retail investor a global unit trust is a good way to start.

DIVERSIFICATION was the buzzword two years ago, when investors who were heavily weighted in Asian equities saw their portfolio sink heavily into the red. During that time, many were saying that the greatest lesson learnt from the 1997/98 Asian crisis was the word 'diversification', which simply means never put all your eggs into one basket.

In the year 2000, the Asian economies are roaring back with vengeance. Fund managers are actively promoting Asian funds again by launching new themes or relaunching existing Asian funds with promotions. Are investors over-weighted in Asian funds again? Have we forgotten our lesson?

Investors must realise that Asia forms a very small portion of the world markets. Going by the MSCI World index – the best representation of the world market – the US has the largest allocation of 50.1 per cent, followed by Europe with 20.4 per cent, Japan with 12.1 per cent and UK with 10.4 per cent. Singapore has only 0.5 per cent weighted in that index.

This implies that investors must have some holdings in the US, Europe and Japan, the three largest and most developed stock market, even though there may be corrections. Also investors must diversify across different asset classes, which are equities, bonds and cash.

But how do you go about it? For the retail investor, one way to get around the problem is to invest through a global unit trust.

A global unit trust is one that invests in equities of many countries, unlike a country or regional fund which is more focused. To reduce risk further, bonds should be included in the portfolio. Bonds would act as a buffer as they thrive during low inflation, low interest rate environment.

Diversification can be achieved either by buying into a bond fund or a balanced fund. Balanced funds invest in both equities and bonds, and usually require a long term view for purposes like funding your retirement. The typical balanced funds have a 'neutral composition' of 60:40 between equities and bonds. (This assumes a fully invested portfolio). In reality the weightings are constantly shifting, depending on the outlook of the fund manager.

Another way to achieve global diversification is to do it on a piecemeal basis. Of course, the investor who opts for this method must be well versed in macroeconomics. He can choose from a range of single country funds to form his overall global portfolio and over-weight countries that he is confident will have continuing growth. The best part of such a method is that you do not have to worry what stock to buy – just focus on the macro picture, i.e. the economies and let the fund manager do the stock selection for you.

Furthermore, you are in control of your investment as to which country to over-weight and are not subject to the fund manager's country allocation as in a global equity fund. On the flipside, if you change allocation too often, there will be charges incurred which will eat into your returns. However, the lay investor may be confused by the sheer number of authorised unit trusts. How does one choose from the more than 160 unit trust offered by 27 asset management companies? Not forgetting that you should diversify your investments across various asset classes and countries.

Ultimately, the objective is to achieve the lowest possible risk with the best return in your portfolio. This is called portfolio optimisation. Fortunately, some banks and stockbroking houses here provide investor with such a service.

Currently, investors can choose from 16 global equity funds, 15 global bond funds and 15 global balanced funds. With an initial investment from $1,000 to $5,000, investors can get access to global diversification, including various asset classes.

Returns for global equities fund have not been disappointing. A survey by S&P Micropal shows that the average one year and two year returns for global equities are 38.66 per cent and 34.43 per cent respectively. What is more impressive is the three-year average return of 51.32 per cent (which isn't bad for a global fund).

While past performance is no guarantee of future performance, we believe that by understanding marcoeconomics and selecting the right fund, investors can achieve proper diversification and returns.

The choice of a fund really depends on your investment objective and risk tolerance. While equities tend to provide better returns, the trade-off is, of course, higher risk. So whether you want to go for a global fund or mix and match your own portfolio depends on how knowledgeable you are as an investor. Also remember that unit trusts are medium to long-term investments. Be prepared to sit tight and refrain from getting in and out just because markets are unfavourable.

The benefits from global diversification of investment risk are simply too large to be ignored. Investors must proceed boldly with global diversification with the view that many investors around the world have already proved that it works. Finally, global investing makes sense as long as one follows a sensible long-term strategy. In fact, given today's economic climate, global investment is necessary and should form a core holding in your investment portfolio.

28 Know Your Risk-Free Return
The Business Times, 13 February 2004

> Absolute return is not all about investment return, you should also consider what you would be getting if no risk is taken.

INVESTORS often look simply at potential return and invest without taking risk-free returns into consideration. They don't really bother about the risk-free rate they are getting. A simple reason I can think of is that the risk-free rate is just too small for them to consider, or they are not aware of the risk-free rate they are entitled to.

But first of all, what is a risk-free rate? The proper definition of a risk-free instrument is threefold. First, there is no default risk at all. This means the instrument will fully keep its promise to pay. Second, the standard deviation (a statistical measurement for risk) of the instrument must be zero – that is, there is no risk at all. And third, the rate of the risk-free return is known. That means the return is announced in advance – for example, 2 per cent per annum.

How can risk-free rates help us? Well, we all know that the safest place to keep our money is in the bank or somewhere else that is secure. But in reality this is where you get the lowest return, which many investors are not happy with. Hence, the principle of high risk, high return and low risk, low return comes into the equation.

The next question is: Do we have any risk-free instruments in Singapore? Of course. We have bank interest, CPF interest that is 2.5 per cent for the Ordinary Account and 4 per cent for the Special Account, and Singapore Government bonds – all of which are good examples of risk-free instruments. To me, a risk-free return is akin to doing nothing but still getting paid a little.

Many investment concepts, risk-free is an important element to consider. When looking at the return on an investment, investors should not be happy just to look at the risk-free return – that is, the return I could have earned if they did not take any risk.

Hence, the proper way to look at returns is to use the investment return and subtract the risk-free rate and come up with what we call the 'excess return'. It's the return in excess of the risk-free that we should be looking at. Not the absolute return.

All of us understand that investing our money outside a risk-free instrument is risky. So to invest outside a risk-free instrument we want to be compensated further for taking extra risk. Otherwise, it does not make sense for me to forego the risk-free and assume market risk, as we all know that the market is uncertain. This extra return is to compensate me for taking extra risk and it's called the risk premium.

Before investing in any instrument, you should ask yourself what the expected return should be. You should have in mind a required rate of return for the risk taken. The simple concept is to add the risk-free return to the risk premium. Then at least you will know the expected return on the investment before actually investing in it.

Hence, in investment world, we have a well-known concept called Capital Asset Pricing Model or CAPM in short. This model helps investors understand returns that take risk-free return and market risk into consideration. The basic formula for CAPM is:

Required rate of returns (K) = Risk free + β (Return of the market - Risk free).

Financial theory says riskier assets must offer higher expected returns and assets pricing models quantify this. This model says a stock is risker the more closely its price moves with prices in the market as a whole. The appropriate measure of risk is therefore the degree of a stock's co-movement with the market, which is summarised by a measure called beta or β.

This postulates a linear relationship between an asset's beta (a measurement of market risk) and expected return. In the CAPM, good times and bad times are captured by the return on the market. The performance of the market as captured by a broad-based index as acts as a surrogate indicator for the state of the economy.

To have a better understanding, I hope the following example will clearly demonstrate the concept. Say you are approached by a fund distributor who recommends that you invest using your CPF Special Account (SA). You know that the

SA pays 4 per cent per annum. To me this is a risk-free return. In other words, leaving the money in the SA and getting 4 per cent for doing nothing is no risk. But if I were to transfer my SA money into another product, there would be a risk. Obviously, I would not be happy if the fund's return is less than 4 per cent. Because I have taken extra risk, I expect a higher return. Using the basic formula of CAPM, we can input the numbers to see what my expected return should be. (Assuming the market return is 6.3 per cent and β is 1.13).

K = 4 per cent + 1.13 (6.3 per cent − 4 per cent) = 6.59 per cent.

Hence, I will be satisfied if the investment return is 6.59 per cent or higher. If the number is lower than 6.59 per cent, it's not worth taking the extra risk. It can also be seen that the higher the β – that is, market risk – the higher the return. So if the β is 1.5, then the required rate of return would be 7.45 per cent. This captures the high risk, high return concept.

Now we have a complete measurement of return that captures the risk-free and the risk premium. This is how returns should be measured.

Happy investing.

29 Time to Change Strategy
The Business Times Weekend, 17 October 2009

> Investors understand the reasons for investing for the long term especially in a prolonged bear market. However, the temptation to change strategy can be strong when the market rebounds. It's wiser to stay with the familiar and adopt a balanced approach for the long term.

HAVING gone through the financial crisis, many of my clients have expressed a desire to change their approach to investing. They are considering abandoning their long-term approach in favour of more active investing.

At a seminar I conducted, a member of the audience asked me if he should sell his stocks or hold on to them, now that the market had rebounded strongly. While he wanted to realise the profit, he did not want to miss out on a further possible upside. When I asked if he was trying to time the market, he replied that there was nothing wrong with timing the market. He said even the Government of Singapore Investment Corporation (GIC) times the market and manages to cap further losses on its portfolio. More significantly, he added, this was the first time that the GIC was using market timing as opposed to its long-term view on investments.

The stock market is made up of bulls and bears. Some investors reckon quality companies are cheap now and warrant a buy, while others anticipate a double dip and are looking to sell. So how do we manage this buy-sell decision?

A rule of thumb that many investors use is to sell at least enough to recover the initial cost of your investment. You simply sell part of your holding to lock in a profit; that way, you are gambling only with your gain.

My experience as a stock dealer allows me to understand how professional investors make such decisions. Usually, they decide based on their assessment of the company concerned, the economy, the political environment, interest rates and market conditions. They are often called 'fundamentalists' and are macro-focused. These people are very skilful and trained to sniff out good stocks based on fundamentals. I call them 'skills-based' investors.

When analysing stocks, fundamentalists fully understand the underlying fundamentals of the companies whose stock they buy. These include the markets the companies are in, their balance sheets and even their competitors. Fundamentalists also examine past and present earnings to see how these relate to the number of shares outstanding (earnings per share), not to mention an array of other financial ratios. All these are closely watched numbers among professional investors.

On the other hand, other investors make their decisions based on preset rules. These people are referred to as 'technicians'. They look at volumes, chart patterns, moving averages, relative strength indices, graphs, etc. Technicians have a set of rules to follow. For example, they will buy only when there is an uptrend. As such, I call these people 'rules-based' investors.

In reality, both methods require special skill, experience and knowledge to deliver outstanding results on a consistent basis. To be successful at this, you need to be a full-time stock analyst. If you are working during the day, do you have the time to do the research? Hence, few people succeed in trading the market.

Don't decide on price alone

'Buy-low-and-sell-high' is the ultimate guide to successful stock investing. It is also the reverse of what many investors do. It's not that investors intentionally buy high and sell low. But too often they use price (and, in particular, price movement) as their only signal to buy or sell. Some of you may be smart investors who made the right call recently. But do not overestimate your ability. More often than not, recent gains are mainly attributable to the global stock market rally. At times, if you keep betting on it, you will somehow get it right. Even a broken clock is right twice a day.

During the recent market rally, many companies announced positive news. People get excited about what they read and see, and want a piece of the action. They jump into a stock that is already trading at a premium, and in so doing they buy high.

The other side of the coin is when a stock has fallen. Most investors may want to sell, along with the rest of the market.

If you go by price alone, this can be a bad decision (sell low). There can be many reasons why a stock's price drops and some of them have nothing to do with the soundness of the investment. This is why if you only follow price, you may miss opportunities. After a stock's price has fallen, it can be a great time to buy (buy low), but only if you have done your research.

Experienced traders can make money by jumping in and out of a stock that has caught the public's attention, but this is not a game for the inexperienced — and it is not investing. There is risk involved, and it comes with consequences and other issues that mean most investors should leave this activity to short-term traders.

Studying the fundamentals of a company will enable you to set a target price for when to buy and sell. If you base your decision simplistically on stock price alone, you may — and likely will — make investing mistakes. Remember, if a stock has had a good run-up, it may be time to sell, not buy (sell high). Similarly, if a stock has dropped like a rock, it may be a good time to buy, not sell. The benefit of this approach is that it keeps emotions out of the equation. Some may term this approach as being contrarian.

It has been a painful 12 months for equity investors, but this is not the time to make drastic changes. If you took a long-term approach to investing before, don't abandon that approach now. You probably had a balanced approach for good reason and it will likely serve you and your family well for many years. A long-term approach reduces risk and allows for growth. Yes, it has had bad — even terrible — years. But over your lifetime, such an approach should continue to serve you well.

> If you took a long-term approach to investing before, don't abandon that approach now. You probably had a balanced approach for good reason and it will likely serve you and your family well for many years.

That is why the deputy chairman and executive director of GIC cautioned against reading too much into GIC figures, emphasising that GIC is a long-term investor not distracted by short-term market volatility.

Perhaps it's time to rebalance your stock portfolio. Today, a host of quality companies are still attractive. The trick is to recognise them, take a sober view of your existing holdings and take advantage of any down market to upgrade your portfolio. If you're in doubt, always consult a financial adviser.

30 Stay Invested or Adopt Dollar-Cost Averaging
The Business Times Weekend, 25 April 2009

> Is it worth trying to time your investments? Enough people seem to think so. But if you have created an investment mix that is suitable for your risk tolerance and investment objective, then a bear market shouldn't concern you.

RECENTLY, an investor told me this: "This financial tsunami hurts the global economy, it also hurt my stock holding, my retirement funds, my kids' education fund, my insurance policies, my home value, etc..."

Needless to say, the past 15 months have been by far the most upsetting period of any investor's life. Many are doing a lot of soul-searching about their long-term investment strategies and it's not hard to guess why. When all your 'well-diversified, uncorrelated' asset classes drop all at once and your portfolios lose half their value, it has to leave you scratching your head, wondering if a buy-and-hold, value/growth, large cap/small cap/international, single/multi manager and equities/bond fund allocation is really the prudent approach. Some are even lamenting that asset allocation and diversification does not work anymore. But what does all this tell us? What have we learnt from this incident?

It is important to understand why even the most rigorous back-testing of portfolios did not work during this period.

The reason is simple: no back-testing has allowed for as much stress as markets were under from late 2007 to end 2008. There was simply no historic precedent for markets to be as volatile on the downside as they were in 2007–2008. Thus, back-testing (also called stress testing) that called for maximum falls of, say, 33 per cent simply did not work when markets fell as far and fast as they did in that period.

Of course, there have been other times when the markets fell as far — the early and mid-1997/98 are extremely good examples. But this time round, the daily volatility and unprecedented decline after the failure of the Treasury to rescue Lehman Brothers and the subsequent bailout of AIG were simply not on most investors' radar screens.

This means that investors were not prepared, in terms of volatility, for what has happened. Nor were they prepared for a time when almost all categories of investment collapsed simultaneously: large cap, small cap, value, growth, emerging markets. At the same time, corporate and government bonds fell sharply, as did nearly every commodity, including hedge funds. (Remember, hedge funds are sold on the basis that they are less correlated to stock market movement.) Real estate, both commercial and residential, also fell dramatically. No amount of diversification would have worked to preserve capital, other than having short- and medium-term Treasuries. Even cash at our local banks had to be guaranteed by the government, thereby providing a safety net for depositors.

Another point I would highlight is that the back-testing of data and portfolio propositions did not foresee a massive loss of confidence, thanks to catastrophically wrong business models adopted by US financial institutions. Are those disastrous models an indication that we need to rethink our whole investment approach? Of course, the bear market has hurt millions of investors, but in the end all this pain and suffering is merely a payback for the bullish returns of the past few years. And will investors who stay the course be rewarded for their patience and determination?

One statistical theory argues that after a long period of strong performance, stocks can't avoid going through a bad period, and that's what happened last year.

If the market has been falling for a period of time, there will be some small rebound along the way, as we have witnessed in the past six weeks. However, many pundits are calling it a bear rally. In any case, anyone who is interested in small rallies are those with a short-term view. However, I believe that on a longer-term basis, we all know that the market will rebound.

During a sustained market upswing or downswing, one of the most discredited principles of asset allocation is that of reversion to the mean. This means that, over time, the returns of a given asset class tend to gravitate towards the long-term average for that asset category; hence, the cycles of rising and falling prices that markets experience.

However, when investors have been experiencing some years of abnormally high or low returns, they begin to believe that those returns probably would not get back to the long-term mean of that asset class. They also generally lose sight of the fact that those long-term average returns imply that the asset would, at some point, produce returns as far (and sometimes as often) below the mean as above.

What this suggests is that, as unnerving as recent events have been, history has shown us that the economy will come back and that means the market will, too. Five or ten years from now, people will look back at this time and wish that they had invested more. That is why pundits are calling on investors to either stay invested or adopt dollar-cost averaging to avoid missing the recovery.

So, why didn't asset allocation work last year? As we know, the fundamental reason for not putting all our eggs in one basket is to reduce risk and improve investment performance. However, for asset allocation to work, there should be no single asset class that dominates other asset classes year after year. But if you look at the broad asset classes, global market equity was the best performing asset class for three years in a row till 2006.

In such circumstances, investors tend to focus on the outperformance of the most successful asset class. This is a recipe for disaster as the general focus is on the returns component of asset allocation, rather than on the equally important risk management and risk control feature of asset allocation. This reminds me of the bullish China and India markets a few years ago where investors continued to plough new money in these markets even as the markets reached a fresh all-time high week after week. When the market crashed, investors were completely devastated.

Another basic tenet of asset allocation is the expectation that the returns, risk (as measured by standard deviation) and correlation of the asset classes will remain within some reasonable bounds of their historical performance, and that the relationships among these measures will hold true over time.

However, over the years there have been some assets that began to behave like other assets. For example, several types of fixed-income securities may display patterns of returns, standard deviation and correlations of returns that are analogous to those of equity assets such as preference shares. When the correlation between groups of assets is high, it negates the risk reduction benefits of diversification.

However, if you had created an investment mix that suits your risk tolerance and investment objective, then a bear market shouldn't concern you. For instance, if you don't need the money for a few decades, and you are an aggressive investor, you might be invested completely in stocks. There is nothing wrong with that, but you should only be invested this way if you understand and are comfortable with the fact that with significant gains may come significant losses at times. That is just the nature of investing entirely in stocks.

If you become uncomfortable with the losses in your portfolio, it probably means that you aren't invested according to your risk tolerance. This commonly happens when investors get overly aggressive in a bull market and reverse gear once losses start to show up on statements. Avoid the temptation to alter your investments based on what the prevailing markets are doing.

In conclusion, mean reversion is one of many reasons why maintaining a well-diversified portfolio using asset allocation strategies makes sense. By keeping your money in a variety of investments, you'll balance out the inevitable ups and downs across your portfolio and keep a more even keel as you move toward your financial goals.

Happy investing!

31 A Boring Approach that Works
The Business Times Weekend, 20 June 2009

> The mix of investments you choose to put your money into can provide a powerful strategy against huge losses if things go wrong. Keeping a balanced, diversified position instead of timing markets ensures your goals are met and risk is minimised.

MY article "Stay invested or adopt dollar-cost averaging", which was published in *The Business Times* on 25 April this year (see previous article), attracted some criticisms from a reader.

In his opinion, the article — which ended with the statement that "mean reversion is one of many reasons why maintaining a well-diversified portfolio using asset allocation strategies makes sense" — was biased. Advisers, he said, do not address Warren Buffett's statement that "diversification is only required when investors do not understand what they are doing".

He went on to accuse local financial advisory firms of being always bullish, optimistic and talking about V-shaped recoveries, while knowing that the economic outcome is likely to be a painful U or an ugly L. He concluded that as advisers, our objectives are to get people to buy products and put their money with us so we can survive in this industry.

For obvious reasons, he chose to remain anonymous.

I wrote the article as a reminder to readers. I did not expect to receive such a response. But probably, my critic has lost a lot of money in the financial crisis.

What surprises me is that after so many years of well-supported empirical evidence and research showing it is impossible to time the market, there are people who still persist in believing they can time the market perfectly (refer to the Dalbar studies).

Holding cash now may not be such a great idea. If I had followed my critic's advice to stay in cash, I could have ended up a disaster for my clients. Anyone who sold their investments in the first quarter of 2009 and is still holding on to the cash today is in a worse situation than if they had stayed invested.

Advisers advocate diversification or asset allocation in portfolio management to ensure clients never take on more risk than agreed upon. This is because we do not know when the market will turn around. Nor do we have the ability to time the market. That is why diversification is the foundation of all our investment plans.

Numerous studies have shown that people pour money into equities when the market is up, and sell when it goes down — continuously buying high and selling low. This irrational behaviour causes their returns to be substantially less than index returns. Emotions spark illogical investment decisions. And the tendency to overreact can become even greater during times of personal uncertainty or near retirement.

How many of us are like Mr. Buffett, whose investment horizon is long and whose capital is vast? Mr. Buffett knows exactly what he is doing, but our clients don't.

This is precisely the reason for diversification, and it is a long-standing, time-tested and prevalent investment theory that has enabled us to reduce the risks relating to holding and investing in stocks and other financial assets.

As an adviser with more than 20 years' experience, I have seen local financial advisory services mature with time. Having earned the trust of clients to handle huge funds under advice (also known as assets under advice), advisers shoulder a heavy responsibility. The practice of gathering assets without regard for clients' interests is completely unacceptable behaviour.

Of course, there will always be some bad apples around, but the many people I know are dedicated to this profession. Putting their clients' interests first has become an even higher calling since the financial crisis.

I always tell new clients to check their expectations. If they are looking for high returns, they have come to the wrong person. After all, the measure of a successful financial adviser is not how much money he makes for his clients, but whether the clients have been able to meet their financial objectives through his advice.

An adviser needs to provide consistent returns by adopting an investment strategy — a set of rules, behaviours or procedures designed to guide the selection of a portfolio. The strategy will be crafted around the investor's risk-return trade-off. Some investors will prefer to maximise expected returns by investing in riskier assets. Others will prefer to minimise risk. But most will choose a strategy somewhere in between.

This is why we adopt a systematic way of investing. It has been academically proven that a disciplined approach to investing delivers consistent returns.

Several months ago, I was invited to address the audience of a security company in Jakarta. My talk was entitled "Celebrate when the market goes down". Initially, the organisers thought I was crazy. But at the end of the presentation, I received strong feedback from the audience that it is wise to stay invested and adopt a systematic approach to investing. Psychologically, nothing is more depressing than seeing your investments drop in value. But if you invest regularly and have some time before retirement, bear markets can be a beautiful thing.

The systematic approach called dollar-cost averaging is a proven one. When the market falls, you essentially pick up funds or shares at more attractive prices.

If you feel your emotions getting the better of you, think again. A conscious and thoughtful decision to do nothing is still a form of action. As economist Gene Fama Junior says: "Your money is like soap. The more you handle it, the less you'll have it." Isn't this true?

Every historical study I have seen shows the stock market has an upward bias, meaning that in the long term, we can expect positive returns despite bad years here and there. Just as you wouldn't run out and put your home up for sale when prices head south, do not act rashly and sell equities when the stock market goes through a bear cycle. Wait, and think again before you react.

> **Nothing is more depressing than seeing your investments drop in value. But if you invest regularly and have some time before retirement, bear markets can be a beautiful thing.**

If your funds are allocated correctly, you should never have a need to sell equities in a down market cycle. You may merely have to rebalance your portfolio to reflect your risk level. Maintaining a balanced and diversified position takes precedence over following market gyrations, and helps ensure that goals are met and risk is minimised.

This may sound boring, but it works. I always remind clients that their investments should be boring so that their life can be exciting and they can sleep peacefully at night.

32 When an Investor Burns His Finger
The Business Times Weekend, 6 December 2008

> What you select for your portfolio also depends on the kind of investor you are and the amount of time you want to spend finding the appropriate returns. In a bear market, you should take advantage of potential investment opportunities rather than focus on losses.

LAST week, I had a chat with Peter who was very depressed with the performance of his unit trust portfolio. As a self-taught investor, he has been diligently applying many investment strategies such as diversification, asset allocation, rebalancing, and even dollar-cost averaging.

When I analysed his portfolio, I realised that it was well diversified across asset classes, countries and managers. Furthermore, he rebalances his portfolio once a year to keep his overall portfolio risk relatively constant. Financial advisers often advise clients to adopt these investment strategies.

Unfortunately, Peter's portfolio could not withstand the financial turmoil and has declined by more than 59 per cent compared with a year ago. Peter is now frustrated and wonders what to do next. The current state of the financial markets is highly volatile and difficult to predict. The recent failures of some structured products are a testament to this tumultuous market.

Having been in the financial industry for more than 20 years, I've observed investors and their behaviours during difficult times like this. I hope that by explaining why investors behave in a certain manner, you will be able to consciously identify some of these behaviours and better manage your investment decisions.

In Peter's case, I agree that his portfolio is well diversified. However, diversification serves only to minimise risk. Consider the two types of risk that our investments are exposed to: systematic risk and non-systematic risk.

Systematic risk (also called market risk) is a type of risk that is inherent in every market. In general, risks of this nature include interest rate, inflation and currency risks. It also includes events like September 11 and the current financial crisis which impacted all major markets globally. It's impossible to completely avoid this type of risk.

Non-systematic risk includes company specific financial risk, management risk and industry risk. Fortunately, this type of risk can be eliminated by investing in a diversified portfolio consisting of companies across industries and markets.

Researchers have found that people feel the sting of loss twice as acutely as they feel the pleasure of gain. Many investors often make investment decisions by taking into account the latest possible market information. The financial media, through television channels and the newspapers, are devoted to the financial markets worldwide, 24 hours a day and seven days a week.

In recent times, almost every piece of news you read or hear is bad news. Companies are announcing job cuts and forecasting lower revenue. At the same, more people are facing credit problems and bankruptcy is on the rise. The world economy is slowing down and recession has begun in most countries. Such news will inevitably cause investors to focus on losses and foster a tendency to evaluate and analyse their returns frequently. Simply speaking, investors tend to focus on losses rather than take advantage of potential investment opportunities.

But how do the wealthy react to losses? Do they bury their head in the ground and be disappointed? We know that this crisis affects everyone, but what is important is how we react to such losses.

We know that even the super rich suffered paper losses this time round. This includes well-known investors like Bill Gates who lost US$3.2 billion, Warren Buffett who lost US$5.29 billion, and Li Ka Shing who lost about half his wealth. On the contrary, instead of focusing on losses, they are investing even more.

What about Sovereign Wealth Funds? (SWFs are state-owned investment entities with the mandate to invest their country's assets.) As reported in the papers, in October 2008, $16.4 billion in market value was wiped off from Temasek Holding's portfolio. This is based only on 12 Singapore-listed companies that Temasek has significant stake in.

Hence, it is evident that almost everyone who invested in equities is affected. Peter should not be too disappointed with his portfolio performance because no matter how much he diversifies his portfolio, it is difficult to be insulated from the negative global impact. Peter must also recognise that investors never make money when they buy; they only make money when they sell (at the right price). On the same token, investors never really lose money when the market is down; they only lose when they sell (at a loss).

Another observation is that people tend to focus on the performance of individual components, such as a specific unit trust, rather than the overall portfolio. Investors should aim to pursue an asset allocation aligned with their risk appetite. The investment decisions made should be targeted towards the long-term horizon. A well-diversified portfolio doesn't mean that every component will perform well all the time. It is more important that the overall portfolio returns are consistent during good times and bad times. Hence, components of the portfolio should have little correlation with one another.

Most investors, however, want each and every stock of their portfolio to give superior performance all the time. This is not a realistic expectation and can result in 'chasing the hot sectors' behaviour.

I frequently ask my clients: "Can you tolerate seeing somebody else's portfolio doing better than yours?" I remember a client whom I had helped to develop a balanced portfolio. I laid out a careful plan for him by splitting his investment assets into four categories: domestic equities, domestic bonds, international equities and international bonds. This client understood completely what we wanted to achieve with a balanced portfolio.

In the middle of 2007, he called me up. He was quite upset that his investments were under-performing the Straits Times Index (STI). I thought to myself: with only 25 per cent of his assets invested in domestic equities, he could not expect the portfolio to outperform the STI. In fact, one reason why we developed a balanced portfolio was to make sure that it was less risky (volatile) than the STI. Nevertheless, I can understand his anxiety. The last few years have been great for domestic equities, and the media has many times reported that the STI has hit an 'all time high'. My client felt that he was 'missing out' on the action. While his reaction was understandable, this investing mentality is not very useful in making sound investing decisions.

I have also observed that investors tend to believe that events are more predictable than they actually are. For example, looking at past performance leads us to presume prior patterns will persist. If a stock or other asset class did well historically, it will continue to be a star. Those that did not perform will continue to underperform. In Peter's case, the more he reads about the rise of China and India, the more he invests in China and India equities. Unfortunately, most of these markets are currently down.

There are three ways to overcome these mental biases:

- First, take note of how often you update yourself on your investments and how often you follow the stock market.
- Second, make sure that you invest with a long-term perspective and analyse your portfolio as a whole instead of its individual parts.
- Third, seek out the opinions of other investors that you disagree with and see if their opinions have any merit.

In conclusion, investors should not be under the misconception that investing in unit trusts is a cushion against risk. Today, the world stock market is generally in a bearish phase. There is very little that you can do if your investments were made just before the onset of the market downturn. However, it is important that you adopt the right investing mentality so that you can make more rational and wiser investment decisions. Don't focus on the losses. Instead, look for potential opportunities during market lows. Remember what Warren Buffet said: "Buy when there is fear in the market."

33 The Portfolio Strategy and Your Adviser
The Business Times, 11 June 2008

> If you work with a financial adviser to help you with your investments, should you instruct your adviser to change strategy based on your own gut feel? The answer is no. A good adviser often strikes a balance between making tactical changes and cautioning clients about acting on emotions.

A REFERRED client recently consulted me regarding his investment portfolio. After the introductions, he quickly settled down and poured out his woes to me. Listening to him, I began to understand his anxiety and why he urgently needed help.

His story goes like this. In late 2007, he was concerned about the many signs that pointed to a slowdown in the world economy in 2008. He told his financial adviser he wanted to restructure his investment portfolio into a more conservative one, but the adviser resisted his suggestions. By not doing anything, his portfolio suffered losses. He wondered if he should stick with an adviser who seemed only to adopt a buy-and-hold formula. He felt that his portfolio should be actively managed and that he should be given advice regularly to help him navigate the dynamic market conditions.

But as he spoke, this thought went through my mind: if the client had the expertise to predict future market performance, why did he need an adviser in the first place? I told him that looking at the facts, I didn't think the adviser had done anything wrong.

He was stunned by my reply. In fact, I added, I would be more suspicious of advisers who were eager to sell or switch investments. After all, making more buy and sell recommendations could generate additional commissions, or at least make it appear that the adviser is on top of the situation.

Was the adviser wrong in doing nothing? In my opinion, the fact that your adviser doesn't agree with your suggestion to move into more conservative investments doesn't mean that he is lazy or incompetent. In fact, it means quite the opposite. If you were going into 2008 with a diversified portfolio that is in line with your risk appetite, then it seems reasonable that an adviser would caution you against making any big changes.

That's not to say that an adviser should not re-evaluate a strategy in light of market conditions, or even make changes. But I believe a good adviser must strike a balance between making tactical changes to the client's portfolio and cautioning clients about acting on their emotions.

I reminded my new client that we can only accurately assess a situation with the benefit of hindsight. Hardly anyone could have predicted that the stock market would crash in 1987 or that dot.com stocks would melt down in 2000 or that a financial crisis was looming in 1997 or that property would peak in 2007.

I do not believe that restructuring a portfolio just because the client feels that the next year is going to be bad is the right course of action because it is almost impossible to identify accurately which part of the portfolio will be adversely affected. It is unrealistic to expect the financial adviser to predict the market. Even if he was right one time, he would not be able to do it consistently. Think how you would feel if your adviser warned you of an impending downturn and moved you into more conservative investments, only to be wrong.

Since it is unrealistic to always invest at the right moment, what should you do? You should first ask yourself why you are investing. Is it for income, growth or for speculative reasons? In order to structure an appropriate investment portfolio and expect a reasonable return, you need to have a clear set of investment objectives.

As such, your adviser should be exploring your goals with you. He should also understand how much risk you are willing to accept in order to reach your goals. He must also explain how you should react to market downturns along the way. If you haven't had such a conversation with your adviser and if he does not contact you periodically to evaluate your situation, then I don't see how he can give you reasonable advice.

Once your adviser understands your goals and level of risk tolerance, he can put in place an investment strategy. The common foundation for such a strategy should be a diversified investment portfolio that includes a variety of different stocks, bonds or unit trusts.

While the adviser cannot guarantee performance, he should be able to advise you on how that portfolio might perform over the long run. At the very least, he should tell you how the portfolio has performed in good and bad markets in the past by explaining to you the range of returns given the level of risk you are exposed to.

In real life, no strategy is going to go exactly according to plan. Hence, your adviser should be providing periodic reports, perhaps every quarter or even every six months. He should also show you how you are doing in relation to an appropriate benchmark. If your portfolio's performance is not up to expectation, then your adviser should explain why this has happened and discuss whether any rebalancing is required.

A good adviser knows that markets are volatile and that this will naturally upset many investors. So aside from periodic updates, an adviser should make an extra effort to keep in contact with clients during volatile periods. At such times, it is not enough for an adviser to say: "Keep holding on and all will be well." A good adviser should be willing to go over the investment strategy again to make sure that it is still appropriate for your situation. He must also explain why the strategy still applies even if your portfolio is currently suffering a paper loss.

If the adviser discovers that your financial situation has changed or it turns out you have over-estimated the level of risk you can accept, then it makes sense to fine-tune your portfolio. However, if you are constantly making changes to your portfolio, then he probably doesn't have a real strategy for you.

I don't think any client would expect his adviser to have a crystal ball. What clients probably do expect is someone to manage their portfolio and at the very least, to call them when the market goes down to either reassure them or rebalance the portfolio, basically, so that they know their adviser is alert and responsible.

As for diversifying one's portfolio, I have heard the advice that if an individual does nothing else but diversify his portfolio, he will be protected from market downturns. Many were encouraged to do this in late 1995/6 by their advisers, and then were told to 'hold for the long term' while they watched the Asian markets turn negative for three years in a row. Remember, a well-diversified portfolio will not earn you superior returns, but that is not what investors should be seeking. Nobody can be sure where the markets will head in the short term. So the whole strategy is to re-assess your portfolio from time to time and keep your investments in check. Otherwise, diversification alone will be a dangerous strategy.

If you want to take big risks and try to time the market (something very few people can do), don't expect your adviser to make those decisions for you; you'll have to decide on your own. The latest Dalbar studies show that over the 20-year period ended December 2007, the S&P 500 has gained 11.8

per cent a year while the average equity investor would have earned an annualised return of just 4.48 per cent. Why is this so? I believe it's because many investors think they can predict the future. If you don't have a crystal ball, that 11.8 per cent doesn't sound too bad, does it?

Ultimately, when looking for a good adviser, you need to find someone you can trust, who will educate you, set up a proper asset allocation strategy and invest in assets that make sense to you. Be disciplined and consider adopting a regular contribution investment strategy like dollar-cost averaging, and evaluate the strategy periodically. Having considered all the points here, decide whether your adviser meets your expectations. But if you want to replace your financial adviser because he cannot predict the future, then I wish you all the best in your search for another adviser.

> The foundation for an investment strategy is a diversified portfolio that includes a variety of stocks, bonds or unit trusts. The adviser should be able to advise you on how the portfolio might perform in the long run.

34 Shock-Proof Your Portfolio
The Business Times, 20 August 2008

> In order not to be caught off guard when the market turns south, you must have a proper investment strategy so that you will know what to do when the market does turn volatile.

IN the past six months, I've been invited to speak at several investment seminars in the region. During the question-and-answer sessions, I'm often asked what to do with an investment portfolio that is down and falling. Is it best to cut your losses or hang in there? Well, there is no 'one size fits all' answer. Rather, there are ways to avoid such a situation in the first place.

Understandably, stock markets worldwide have been sold down because of relentless negative news on oil prices, the US dollar and the sub-prime mess. This news has caused panic. Strangely enough, even some financial advisers are wondering what to do with their clients' portfolios now that they are down. Of course, this would not have happened had the advisers implemented a proper investment strategy.

What can one do to navigate through volatile economic waters? Before you do anything, you must accept the fact that plunges are part of the bumpy ride that investment markets offer.

Make volatility work for you

Investors without a proper strategy often are fearful when markets turn volatile. But didn't they know that equity markets are intrinsically volatile? If you have a proper investment strategy, you should be comfortable even when the market is extreme. Indeed, you should be happy when it is down because you can buy at a discount. Singaporeans like discounts and sales, but when there is a sale in the stock market, they act the opposite way.

Investors hope the ride will be up all the way, but the reality is that markets fluctuate on a daily basis. Essentially, it is difficult to determine the trend of the stock market. So those who wonder whether to sell now are investors who have no idea of strategy. To me, they may as well go gambling.

There is plenty of research that shows we cannot time the markets. One of the more popular pieces of research is Dalbar's QAIB 2007, which provides evidence to support the argument that there is no advantage in timing markets or picking sectors. It suggests that timing is as good as making a bet, and that the average investor loses significant value.

The research also shows that the average equity investor who played the market between 1986 and 2007 earned an average annual return of only 4.48 per cent, instead of 11.8 per cent available from the S&P 500 if they had stayed invested.

As such, investors should adopt dollar-cost averaging (DCA). This is defined as constant investment in a fund at pre-determined times — you buy more units when the price is low, and fewer when it is high. Over the long term, you will get many more units in the lower price range.

Often, people lack the discipline to save and invest consistently. DCA forces you to adopt a savings plan because you devote a fixed dollar amount to buying units every month or every quarter. Moreover, DCA uses direct debit so you won't feel too much of a financial pinch.

When you adopt DCA, you let the inherent volatility of the market work for you.

> **You should be happy when the market is down because you can buy at a discount. Singaporeans like discounts and sales. But when there is a sale in the stock market, they act the opposite way.**

It's impossible to buy low and sell high all the time. The best solution is DCA, because you will not be caught committing all your money at the high point of a cycle. Of course, you may not be able to make a profit until the next cycle comes along. But averaging the price of your units puts you in the middle price of the cycle, so you can get to enjoy a pretty good upside.

Instead of being stressed out over the volatility of the market, you can rest easy, knowing that your investment plan is working for you in volatile conditions. And that's just what your investments should be doing — giving you more money and less stress.

The balancing act

In rising markets, people often take on more risk than they are suited to. We have seen this over the past three years, when large numbers of investors fell in love with equities and did nothing to their portfolios. Consequently, they ended up with a larger percentage of equities than their risk levels warranted. And when the market declined, they saw their portfolio lose at a faster rate than it rose. To me, this is greed and fear.

Can it be avoided? Yes. A simple approach called rebalancing will take out the greed and fear factor. Unfortunately, many investors think it is a troublesome process. In fact, it is a simple process that will help you bring different asset classes back into a proper relationship following a significant change in one or more classes.

Simply stated, it is returning your portfolio to the proper mix of stocks, bonds and cash when the allocation no longer conforms to your original plan. For example, your initial asset allocation might have been 60 per cent equity, 30 per cent bonds and 10 per cent cash. (See Figure 1 overleaf.)

Due to the bullish stock market, your asset allocation changed to 80 per cent equity, 15 per cent bonds and 5 per cent cash. Accordingly, you should rebalance the portfolio to get back to the initial asset allocation.

You do this by selling 20 per cent of your equity and buying an additional 15 per cent bonds, and keeping 5 per cent cash. If you look carefully, rebalancing requires you to sell assets that are performing well and buy assets that are currently out of

Figure 1 Rebalancing your portfolio

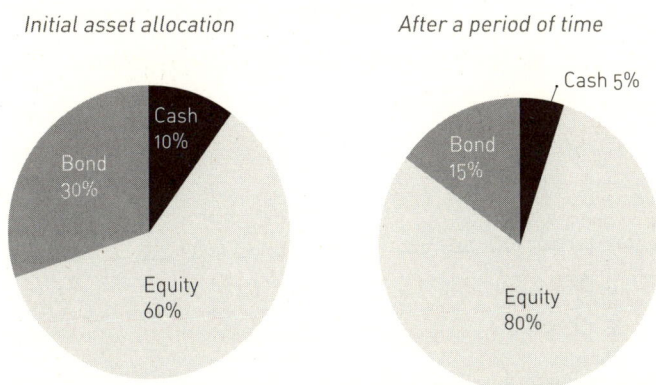

favour. Try thinking of it this way: you are taking profit from your winners and buying other assets that are down. By doing so, you are lowering your risk and achieving higher returns. In fact, you are selling high and buying low.

For example, during the past two years, China has attracted many investors. The investors added to their already over-weighted positions by buying more, assuming the stellar performance would continue indefinitely, and gave little thought to the impact it might have on their portfolio. When the market experienced a sharp fall in late 2007, their investments were pounded more than they had expected.

Remember, rebalancing is an important strategy because you are sticking to your original investment game plan. You should look at your portfolio at least quarterly in terms of rebalancing, and more frequently if you have witnessed a significant shift in allocation of any asset class. This is a critical step in controlling risk.

However, if you have a DCA plan in place, there is less of a need to rebalance your portfolio frequently because each time you invest, whether the market is high or low, rebalancing has already been done for you.

My belief is that the average investor who has a full-time job is better off investing for the long term and ignoring the short-term volatility of markets. Remember, short-term volatility is only important to short-term investors. All you need do is have proper asset allocation with diversification and a disciplined investment strategy, and consistently rebalance your portfolio. As long as you keep your long-term financial goals in mind during both good and bad times, you will generally do better than any short-term trader.

Finally, for financial advisers who have asked me what to do with a client's portfolio, bear in mind that your job as an adviser is not to make your clients rich but to achieve consistent returns so they can achieve their financial objectives. As long as your clients are able to achieve their financial objectives, you have done your job. Therefore, when constructing an investment portfolio for your clients, do ensure that the investment

> **My belief is that the average investor who has a full-time job is better off investing for the long term and ignoring the short-term volatility of markets. Remember, short-term volatility is only important to short-term investors.**

strategies are appropriate and keep in mind the volatility of the market.

Once your clients understand the reasons for investing and the strategies used, they will not mind holding on to a portfolio even when its value is down. A client once told me that his investments should be boring so his life can be exciting. Happy investing!

35 Have Faith in an Old Friend
The Business Times Weekend, 18 October 2008

> Unit trusts are a good way to diversify across asset classes, geographical regions and investment techniques. If you are uncertain, you can start with a relatively small minimum stake. But that is not true for overseas stocks and picking them takes some careful planning.

EARLY this year, Michael consulted me on investing $800,000 for the purpose of wealth accumulation. As a financial adviser, we went through the 'know your client' process such as understanding his risk tolerance, financial objectives and time horizon. Michael had very little experience in investing and this sum to be invested was from his pension. After presenting a financial plan to him, we agreed that $600,000 will be invested in a portfolio of diversified unit trust funds and $200,000 will be left in the bank as deposit for emergency use. After the discussion, we parted with confidence in the plan.

At that time, GIC (Government of Singapore Investment Corporation) and Temasek Holdings announced that they had invested in three major US financial institutions, namely Citibank, UBS and Merrill Lynch. One week later, Michael called to say that his brother-in-law who was working in an American investment bank recommended him to invest directly in the stock market so as to avoid paying the cost of investing in unit trusts. Following GIC and Temasek's investment in the US financial institutions, he invested $600,000 equally in the three banks and the remaining $200,000 in a structured product. He made the decision by himself. As his financial advisor, I certainly wished him all the best in his investments.

Last week, however, I received a call from him. He was very nervous about the developments in the US financial markets. Considering that he invested his savings in the US financial sector, I can understand his anxiety. Having been in the investment line for the past 20 years, I have never seen such volatility in the financial markets. The Dow Jones can move up 1,000 points while the S&P 500 can jump 8 per cent in two days. Last week, the Singapore stock market suffered its worst one-day decline of more than 6 per cent in a single trading day. Whether we like it or not, we are in unprecedented times in the global financial markets.

Not surprisingly, I have received many queries from clients who are worried about what might happen to their investments and retirement plans should their trusted financial institution go belly up. Difficult as it may be, it is nevertheless important to keep things in perspective in such times of crisis. Decisions should be made on the basis of facts and reasons, not on emotions and fears. Should you panic and pull out from your investments immediately, you may very well end up in a worse position than before. In the context of Michael's case, I would like to address some lessons that we can learn from it.

The most important lesson is the need to diversify your portfolio. Michael did not diversify his investment portfolio and put all his eggs in one basket — the entire $600,000 was invested into the US market. Worse still, his investment was entirely in the financial sector alone. If Michael had diversified his portfolio across countries and sectors, his losses might not have been so large. Furthermore, by investing in direct equities, and in a single country and in a single sector, Michael increased his portfolio investment risk tremendously. This mistake unfortunately cost him 60 per cent of his investment.

Another lesson is not to follow the 'experts' blindly. Just because GIC and Temasek Holdings invested into these banks, it doesn't mean that everyone should follow suit. As individual investors, our financial resources are more limited than the big players. In addition, the playing field is different. GIC invested into Citi Group Convertible stocks, not its ordinary shares. As a Sovereign Wealth Fund, GIC had better bargaining power to negotiate a favourable arrangement for investing in the shares. Also, if Michael had done some research on Temasek Holdings, he would probably not have put all his savings into one sector. Temasek had invested 40 per cent of its portfolio in the financial services sector and less than 23 per cent of its portfolio was invested in the US. The diagrams below reveal Temasek's sector and country allocation as of 30 March 2008.

At this point, we distinguish unit trust investments and direct equities. In a unit trust investment, some form of

Figure 2 Temasek's Portfolio

Sector Allocation

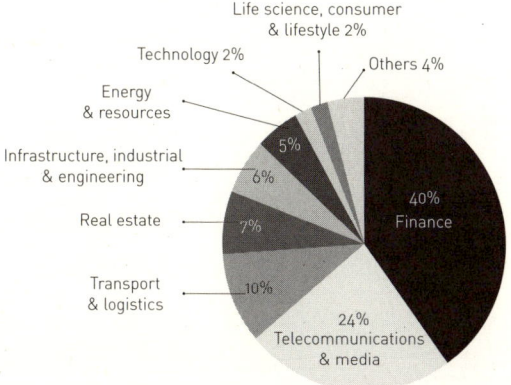

Country Allocation

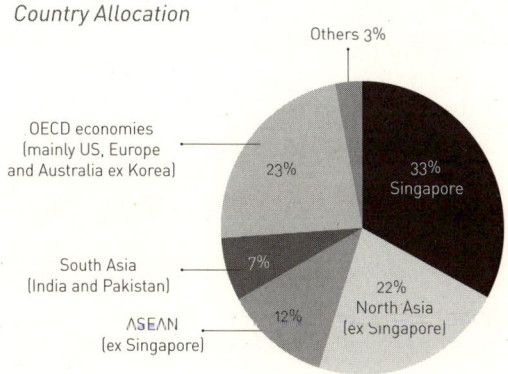

diversification has already been made and investors are better protected against the different type of companies and sector risks in the stock market. As the stock universe is very big, most fund managers invest in hundreds of stocks. Also, for most unit trusts, the maximum exposure to any one stock cannot exceed 10 per cent of the portfolio. This means that investors are better protected against the downfall of any one stock. For example, even if a fund manager has invested in Lehman Brothers or AIG, the impact to the portfolio will be smaller. As individual investors, our investment capability is limited to a small number of stocks. A downfall in one stock can certainly have a huge impact on our portfolio if we are invested in a small pool of stocks. I certainly don't want to wake up in the middle of the night worrying about who will be the next to go bankrupt. Unless you have the financial muscle to invest like a fund manager, you should consider unit trusts over direct equities.

Michael's story does not end here. In addition to his investment disaster, the remaining $200,000 was invested in a five-year structured product with capital protection. This type of product, however, has poor liquidity and high penalty for early redemption. In my years of experience, I have not recommended structured products to my clients. While structured products sound good to the ordinary investor, they may be too complex to adequately grasp. No matter what the investment, it is important for investors to fully understand the financial risks and potential losses arising from their investment. In fact, in other countries, structured products have been criticised for not revealing how the product cost is reached. In other cases, many investors complained about the lack of transparency because they did not know how their returns were being calculated.

In the midst of the tumultuous financial market, I received a letter from a financial institution declaring their exposure to Lehman Brothers. I was shocked when I realised that its capital protected funds had an exposure of up to 29 per cent in Lehman Brothers while the exposure of most bond funds was only between 0.9 per cent and 5.41 per cent. The reason for this high exposure to a single company was probably because of the capital protection needed at maturity. For Michael, I hope he did not lose this part of the money as well.

Looking back into history, the US market has survived the Great Depression and World War II. Asia survived the Asian financial crisis in 1997. The bankruptcy of the 'Wall Street big boys' is definitely painful and shocking, but those who survive will come out stronger, leaner and meaner. While the pain is immediate, it will eventually heal and markets will start to pick up again.

That being said, my point remains that unit trusts continue to be one of the best methods of investing in overseas markets. Unless you are a professional trader, investing in direct equities overseas may not be a good idea due to the time required, brokerage commission, and also the substantially higher information and time risk of having the need to keep in touch with overseas news and, not to forget, the foreign exchange risk.

To me, it is wiser to invest in simple and transparent products. Traditional assets like equity and fixed income are easier to understand in terms of the risk-reward trade-off. Unless you have a sophisticated investment objective, such as principal protection with upside exposure, it may be better to invest in traditional asset classes. Finally, one of the best ways to reduce risk is to diversify across securities, across assets, across managers, and across markets.

> In unit trust investment, some form of diversification has already been made and investors are better protected against the different types of companies and sector risks in the stock market.

> If you become uncomfortable with the losses in your portfolio, it probably means that you aren't invested according to your risk tolerance. This commonly happens when investors get overly aggressive in a bull market and reverse gear once losses start to show up on statements. Avoid the temptation to alter your investments based on what the prevailing markets are doing.

> If your funds are allocated correctly, you should never have a need to sell equities in a down market cycle. You may merely have to rebalance your portfolio to reflect your risk level. Maintaining a balanced and diversified position takes precedence over following market gyrations, and helps ensure that goals are met and risk is minimised.

36 Stock Investing not Always a Gamble
The Sunday Times, 18 July 2010

For starters, the odds are better – if you do your homework before making your picks.

I had a recent conversation with a friend who visited casino and insisted that investing is stocks was similar to gambling. I find it puzzling but I guess some people like to think that way.

Most of us would agree that gambling is a zero-sum game, but is that so for stock investing?

It could be that they don't understand what is a zero sum game is. Or maybe they believe that the market magically creates wealth and the wealth is just passed on from one investor to another.

My understanding of a zero-sum game is this. Let's say there are two or more players in a game. When it is over, there would be winners and losers. The points awarded to the winners exactly match the points lost by the losers.

For example, in the game of poker, some players leave with more money than they started with. But the fact is, every dollar they win is a dollar lost by another player.

This means that one's winnings come from other players' losses or that one's losses become other players' winnings.

At times, you win some games and at other times, you lose some games. But when the day is done, the sum of your winnings and losses is your actual result for the day. If you have lost in the game, nothing can change that fact, because a loss is a loss.

Another point to note is that in casino gambling, no matter how you play the game, the odds are always in the house's favour. We have heard stories of people who have won thousands of dollars, but the fact is you cannot expect to win all the time. In theory, the house can be among the losers at any given time, but gaming is generally profitable because the house typically wins much more than it loses.

Some financial instruments, particularly derivatives, are in fact zero-sum game. Instruments such as options and future contracts are good examples (excluding costs). For every person who gains in a contract, there is a counterpart who loses by exactly the same amount.

I can think of reasons why people have the misconception that the stock market is a zero-sum game. In stock investments, there is a buyer for each seller and a seller for each buyer so each cancels the other and everything is equal. But isn't so.

The reality is that wealth can be created in a stock market. Furthermore, in stock investing, the investor has the odds in his favour.

Most of us invest with the expectation that our portfolio will increase in value overtime. The reason is that the stock market has historically performed an average of 8 per cent to 10 per cent each year.

Of course, there is an element of risk inherent in buying and selling shares, but a savvy investor can reduce it to a relatively safe level.

So if investors don't do due diligence to ensure that they understand the business or company they are investing in, then they deserve to lose part or all of the capital. And this is tantamount to gambling. I believe that the only time stock investing can be considered as gambling is when you are trading in the short term. This is because it is virtually impossible to predict the near term performance of a stock.

This reminds me of the time I was a stock dealer during the bullish technology rally. At that time, I thought I was pretty smart investor. It took me a few months before I realised I was gambling by which time my luck had run out.

Were my losses some other player's winning? No, because all the technology stock crashed to the tune of 70 percent. There were no winners. All were losers and wealth evaporated into thin air.

Thus, I learnt a valuable lesson in the stock market. If you stay invested for the long term, the odds of making money are in your favour and this is not to the detriment of everyone else in the game. On average, over time, those who remain invested in the stock market win.

If you think you can be rich by constantly playing in the casino, think again. There is no lesson that teaches you a preferred technique to pull a slot machine's handle. There are no skill to master in picking random number – otherwise, it wouldn't be called random.

Even in table games, like blackjack, the odds of success are always on the house's side and nothing can change this truth.

Having said all this, I am not discouraging anyone from playing in the casino, enjoying the spin of a roulette wheel or the pull of the slot machine. But bear in mind that they are all exciting for a fleeting moment.

The most dangerous situation you can possibly be in, is gambling when you think you are investing. Just remember this: We don't gamble to make money, we gamble for pure enjoyment.

ABOUT THE AUTHOR

Dr Ben Fok is an industry veteran with more than 30 years' experience in the financial services industry. He was an investment adviser for eight years before joining the stock broking industry as a dealer for five years. He joined the financial advisory industry in 2003. He is currently the Chief Executive Officer of Grandtag Financial Consultancy (Singapore) Pte Ltd, a financial advisory company licenced by the Monetary Authority of Singapore.

Dr Fok is a Certified Financial Planner (CFP®), Chartered Financial Consultant (ChFC®) and Trust and Estate Practitioner (TEP), and he has a doctorate from the University of Canberra. He is also an associate lecturer at a local university for graduate and undergraduate programmes.

Dr Fok is much sought after for his expertise and wealth of knowledge in the financial industry. He has been on television and radio talk shows and has also contributed articles to *The Sunday Times*, *The Business Times* and other financial magazines. He is the co-author of **Make Your Money Work For You** (Marshall Cavendish, 3rd Ed, 2011).